How Typography Happens

ARE WE TO READ

BACKWARDS?

OR,

What is the Best Print for the Eyes?

[ONE SHILLING.]

Cover design of an imaginative booklet about the relationship between type and meaning, published by Field & Tuer, Ye Leadenhalle Presse, London, dated 1884. The frontispiece, using a double impression, shows what type would look like in a train going at 'a mile a minute!'

How Typography Happens

Ruari McLean

The British Library

and

Oak Knoll Press

For Catriona at Sanquhar

First published 2000 by

The British Library
96 Euston Road
London NW1 2DB
UK

and

Oak Knoll Press
310 Delaware Street
New Castle
DE 19720
USA

Library of Congress Cataloging-in-Publication Data
McLean. Ruari.
   How typography happens/Ruari McLean.
      p. cm.
   Includes bibliographical references and index.
   ISBN 1-884718-90-6 (cased) -- ISBN 1-58456-019-3 (pbk.)
   1. Graphic design (Typograhy)--Europe, Western--History. 2. Graphic design
   (Typography)--United States--History. 3. Type and type-founding--Europe,
   Western--History. 4. Type and type-founding--United States--History. 1. Title.

   Z124.M44 2000
   686.2'2--dc21   99-089050

British Library Cataloguing-in-Publication Data
A CIP Record is available from The British Library

ISBN 0-7123-4634-1 (BL cased)
ISBN 0-7123-4642-2 (BL paperback)
ISBN 1-884718-90-6 (Oak Knoll cased)
ISBN 1-58456-019-3 (Oak Knoll paperback)

Designed and typeset by Nicholas Jones with David McLean
at Strathmore Publishing Services, London N7
in Fred Smeijers 'Renard' typeface
Printed in England by St Edmundsbury Press, Bury St Edmunds

Contents

Preface

The text of these lectures, delivered in Cambridge some sixteen years ago, has had a little tidying-up for publication in book form. Unfortunately the slides used to illustrate the lectures were found in 1998 to have completely disappeared, and many of the books used for making them are no longer in my possession: the illustrations are consequently nearly all new. Many are reduced from their original printed size, and are now all shown in monochrome.

In preparing the text for lectures and this book, I have been greatly helped by editorial advice from the late Sem Hartz, and also from my friends James Mosley, Fernand Baudin, John Dreyfus, and Herbert Spencer, to whom I am most grateful.

I am also especially grateful to Nicholas Jones and my son David McLean for their careful work on the production of the book and for making the index.

My gratitude, too, to David Way at the British Library, without whose vision and support this book would not have been published.

RUARI McLEAN
Sanquhar 1999

ONE

Britain and America

My intention in these Sandars Lectures delivered at the University of Cambridge in 1983 was to explore the gradual tendency of the word 'typography' to mean 'typographic design', and the emergence of the typographer as a professional in his own right. It is only very recently that this has happened. When I started my own career as a learner in the Shakespeare Head Press in Oxford, shortly before the Second World War, typographers certainly existed – Bruce Rogers in the USA and Stanley Morison in England, for example – but there was no recognized way of becoming a typographer, there were no recognized qualifications, there was no profession. That all happened after 1945. You can now get a degree – even a university degree – in typography although at the end of the twentieth century there are still I think only two British professors of typography. But even today the word 'typography' is ambiguous: it has a different meaning in the United States. When my translation of Jan Tschichold's book *Typographische Gestaltung* was published in Canada under the title of *Asymmetric Typography*, I was working in London, Tschichold designed the book in Switzerland, and the book itself was produced in Toronto: it owed its publication not to a publisher, but to the courage and imagination of a firm of Toronto typesetters called Cooper & Beatty. The verso of the title page was compiled in Toronto, approved by Tschichold in Basel, and was never seen by me until I had a copy of the book in my hands, when I was astonished to read the phrase 'Typography by Cooper & Beatty Ltd', meaning of course that they had set the type. And a page from that lively American periodical *Upper & Lower Case*, dated September 1982, had the same meaning (*U & LC*, Sept. '82, p.62).

This essay really starts with an extraordinary book, *Mechanick Excercises on the Whole Art of Printing*, by an extraordinary man, Joseph Moxon, who was a contemporary of Samuel Pepys. Moxon is mentioned three times in the Diary, but I think they never met. Moxon was a printer, a globe- and map-maker, and a mathematician, who in 1660 became Hydrographer to the King. Pepys mentions Moxon three times in his Diary. Here is the mention for 8 September 1663:

> Dined at home with my wife, it being washing day; we had a good pie, baked of a leg of mutton. And then to my office and then abroad; and among other places, to Moxon's and there bought a payre of Globes, cost me £3 10s. – with which I am well pleased, I buying them principally for my wife, who hath a mind to understand them – and I shall take pleasure to teach her. But here I saw his great window in his dining-room, where there is the two Terrestrial Hemispheres, so painted as I never saw in my life, and nobly done and to good purpose – done by his own hand.

Pepys later commissioned two globes for his own office – writing 'which will be very handsome – but cost money'.

Pepys mentions Moxon's book *Mechanick Excercises*, which was, according to the Preface in Davis & Carter's edition of it, 'by forty years the earliest manual of printing in any language, and it put in writing a knowledge that was wholly traditional'. Actually, we now know that it was not quite the earliest manual of printing, there were some German ones earlier.

To come back to this word 'typography' and its various meanings, we find that the very first sentence of Moxon's Preface begins with the words 'Before I begin with *Typographie*, I shall say some-what of its Original Invention' – here he used the word Typography as more or less synonymous with printing; but it is not quite synonymous: he means a bit more than just printing: he means what we might call 'The art of printing'. Further on in Moxon's preface occurs the famous phrase which I shall

To the Right Reverend Father in GOD, *JOHN*
Lord Bishop of *Oxford*, and Dean of *Christ-Church*;
And to the Right Honourable Sir *LEOLINE*
JENKINS Knight, and Principal Secretary of
State; And to the Right Honourable Sir *JOSEPH*
WILLIAMSON Knight; and one of His Majesties
most Honourable Privy-Council.

Right Honourable.

Y OUR *ardent affections to promote* Typographie
has eminently appeared in the great Charge you
have been at to make it famous here in England;
whereby this Royal Island stands particularly obliged
to your Generous and Publick Spirits, and the whole
Common-Wealth of Book-men throughout the World, to
your Candid Zeal for the promulgation of good Learning.
  Wherefore I humbly Dedicate this Piece of Typographie *to your Honours; and as it is (I think) the first*
of this nature, so I hope you will favourably excuse small
Faults in this Undertaking; for great ones I hope there
are none, unless it be in this presumptuous Dedication;

An early use of the word 'Typography', in the dedication in Joseph Moxon's
Mechanick Exercises on the Whole Art of Printing, 1683–4, described in these pages.

quote later, but before that, here are Moxon's two previous paragraphs, which are less well known.

Moxon is debating whether printing – or typography – is an art or a science, and brings in Dr Dee, and Vitruvius, and their claims that architecture is a mathematical science. Moxon then says 'Upon the consideration of what he [Vitruvius] has said in behalf of *Architecture* I find that a *Typographer* ought to be equally qualified with all the Sciences that becomes an *Architect*, and then I think no doubt remains that *Typographie* is not also a Mathematical Science.'

> For my own part, I weighed it well in my thoughts, and find all the accomplishments, and some more of an *Architect* necessary in a *Typographer*: and though my business be not Argumentation, yet my Reader, by perusing the following discourse, may perhaps satisfy himself, that a *Typographer* ought to be a man of Sciences.

Then comes the familiar – yet astonishing – definition.

> By a *Typographer*, I do not mean a *Printer*, as he is Vulgarly accounted, any more than Dr *Dee* means a *Carpenter* or *Mason* to be an *Architect*: But by a *Typographer*, I mean such a one, who by his own Judgement, from solid reasoning with himself, can either perform, or direct others to perform from the beginning to the end, all the Handy-works and Physical Operations relating to *Typographie*.

Now that definition of typography, made over 300 years ago, is very beguiling. It has often been quoted as a good – indeed the best – description of what a typographer's function is today. We like especially that bit about 'by his own judgement, from solid reasoning with himself'. But we tend to forget that what Moxon is really talking about is 'the Handy-works and Physical operations' and it is those that he proceeds to describe in detail. It is a manual for craftsmen. He does not talk about design. He nowhere mentions such a thing as a layout – although, as we learned from Adrian Wilson's researches, printers used layouts at least as early as the *Nuremberg Chronicle* of 1493 and probably earlier.

Moxon's first section on the Handy-works begins with the words: 'I shall begin with the Office of a *Master-Printer*, because (as aforesaid) he is the Director of all the Work men, he is the Base (as the *Dutchmen* properly call him) on which the Workmen stand, both for providing Materials to Work withal, and successive variety of Directions how and in what manner and order to perform that Work.' There follows a description of what the Master Printer must provide in terms of space, light, furniture, etc.; there is no mention of aesthetic, or design, direction.

Later in the book we come to Moxon's instructions for Compositors, and there is a section entitled 'Some Circumstances a good *Compositer* considers and observes in *Composing*'. He begins well with: 'A good *Compositer* is ambitious as well to make the meaning of his Author intelligent to the *Reader*, as to make his Work show graceful to the Eye, and pleasant in Reading: Therefore if his Copy be Written in a Language he understands, he reads his *Copy* with Consideration; that so he may get himself into the meaning of the *Author*.' That is very good, very sensible. He then goes on to discuss the arrangement, or as he calls it, 'The ordering and humouring' of a title-page. It is too long to quote here, it simply reflects the conventional practice of his day; it perhaps surprisingly does not mention the use of either ornament, illustration, or colour, and it is not illustrated. I think that Moxon would not have got his degree in typography at the London College of Printing. He does however give a lot of advice on the important but today often neglected art of punctuation, and here is one remarkable short passage: 'If the Emphasis bear hard upon the Word to be exprest as well as the Thing to be exprest, it ought to begin with a *Capital*. I shall bring for instance an Observation I made about forty years ago [the editors point out that he would then have been 17 years old and almost certainly in Holland] on the word *That*, viz. that that Word may be reiterated five times, and make good sense.' [Can a sentence including five consecutive 'thats' make sense?] Here is Moxon's: 'That that That that That Man would have stand at the beginning of the *Line* should stand at the end; it will, by toning and laying Emphasis on the middlemost That become good Sense. Now all the thats ought to be *Set* in *Italick*, and the middlemost That ought to begin with a *Capital*, because it is both the Thing and Word.' Moxon's *Mechanick Excercises* was, as we have seen, the first of all the printed Manuals (at least in Britain) and was the model, or an important source, for nearly all the subsequent ones for two hundred years. A list of printer's Manuals published up to 1850, compiled by Philip Gaskell, Giles Barber, and Georgina Warrilow, was printed in the *Journal of the Printing Historical Society* No. 4 in 1968, and lists 23 in English, 19 in French, 23 in German, and one in Spanish. I cannot claim to have read many of these Manuals, but I believe I am correct in thinking that in every one of them, as in Moxon, if the design of the title-page is mentioned, it is assumed that this is the responsibility of the compositor, and no mention is made of such a thing as a layout. That goes also for many much later printer's manuals, such as the important *The American Printer – a Manual of Typography* by Thomas MacKellar, first published in 1866, of which the 16th edition appeared in Philadelphia in 1886; and Charles Jacobi's *Printing. A Practical Treatise on the Art of Typography*, published in London in 1890, both of which publications contain even less about what may be called the aesthetics of typography than Moxon. We will return to Jacobi later. And in 1870, John Southward published *A Dictionary of Typography and its Accessory Arts* – in which you can look in vain for any entry at all that gives information on how books were, or ought to be, designed.

So 'typography' in the printers' manuals up to and throughout the nineteenth century still means only 'printing' – or 'printing as an art'. How a book looks, in its details, is still assumed to be the compositor's job.

Yet this was not so.

The greatest printed books of history – and I mean great in terms of their typographic design – the books of Jenson and Aldus and Blado and Simone de Colines and Jean de Tournes just for a start – were not designed by compositors. The books of Baskerville and Fournier le Jeune and Bodoni were not designed by compositors – they were designed by artists who were printers, or printers who were artists. To come closer to our own period, to enter the nineteenth century, the books published by, for example, William Pickering and John Philp, were not designed by compositors. Here, however, there is a change: they were not designed by artist-printers either, although the printers certainly must have helped: they were designed by the publishers, by Pickering himself, and Philp; and I am sure that other publishers such as James Burns and Van Voorst also designed their own books. We know that Pickering was responsible for the appearance of his books, because first of all their style is highly distinctive, and secondly we can compare the style of the printers he employed when they worked for other publishers. There was a great collaboration of

THE

AMERICAN PRINTER:

A Manual of Typography,

CONTAINING

PRACTICAL DIRECTIONS FOR MANAGING ALL DEPARTMENTS OF A PRINTING OFFICE,

AS WELL AS

Complete Instructions for Apprentices:

WITH SEVERAL USEFUL TABLES,
NUMEROUS SCHEMES FOR IMPOSING FORMS IN EVERY VARIETY,
HINTS TO AUTHORS, ETC.

By THOMAS MACKELLAR, PH.D.

FIAT LUX.

PHILADELPHIA:
THE MACKELLAR, SMITHS & JORDAN CO.
1887.

Another use of the word 'Typography' in the title-page of Thomas MacKellar's *The American Printer*, Philadelphia, 1887. Original page size: 192 × 116 mm. MacKellar, Smiths and Jordan were absorbed in 1892 by the American Typefounders Co.

design between Pickering and his main printer Charles Whittingham the younger, but the lead came from Pickering.

That is one of the first steps towards the emergence of the specialized typographer, who is neither printer nor publisher. Another step becomes evident in the career of Joseph Cundall, who was born in 1818, did some training as a printer, worked for a bookseller, by the age of 22 had written his first book (*Tales of the Kings of England*, published by Tilt in 1840), at the age of 23 became a publisher, and at the age of 30 or 31 went bankrupt. After that, he became in effect a packager, in the modern publishing phraseology; he put up ideas for books to other publishers, and edited, designed, and produced them, often with his own monogram on the title-page or verso. In one sense, he might be called the first professional freelance book designer; but we have very little documentation of these activities, and while he certainly conceived and planned books which depended on their appearance – they were usually, but not always, gift books, profusely illustrated – I believe that having set the style, he probably left the typographic details to the printer, and that, I suppose, meant the compositor.

In the same period, i.e. the middle of the nineteenth century, we begin to see many other examples of that new kind of creature, known to us later as 'commercial artists', who were forerunners of the graphic designers of today. Perhaps the two best known examples were the architect Owen Jones and the artist John Leighton. Owen Jones was responsible for the interior colour scheme of the Great Exhibition of 1851, the Crystal Palace, and gave up architecture almost entirely to concentrate on creating designs for illuminated books produced by the new process of chromo-lithography, printed at first in his own press. He also designed stationery and playing cards for De la Rue, he designed wallpapers, some of which are

Title-page of Jean de Tournes' *Quadrins historiques de la Bible*, 1558. 160 × 112 mm. 'Quadrins' is probably an older form of 'quatrains', i.e. a type of four-line stanza. The first word of the two lines in italic, 'reuuz', is in modern French 'revus', English 'revised'. The title-page border is a woodcut, and was used by de Tournes for about five other works. The border may have been designed by Bernard Salomon (c. 1506–61), who produced the woodcut illustrations in *Quadrins historiques*. (Courtesy Dr Ulrike Morét, National Library of Scotland.)

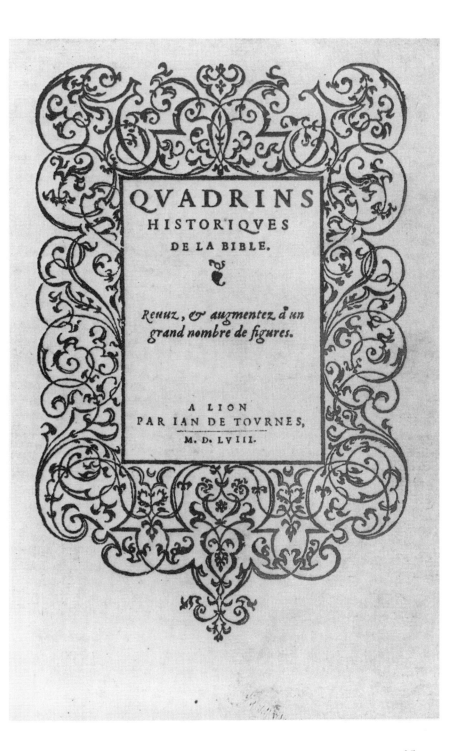

QVADRINS
HISTORIQVES
DE LA BIBLE.

Reueuz, & augmentez d'un grand nombre de figures.

A LION
PAR IAN DE TOVRNES,
M. D. LVIII.

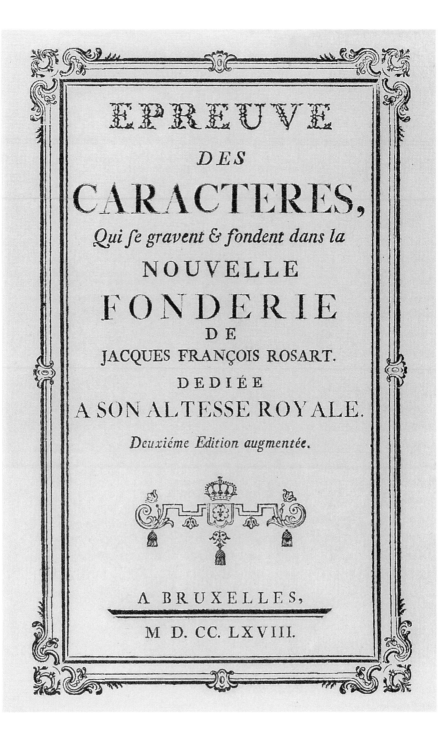

EPREUVE

DES

CARACTERES,

Qui se gravent & fondent dans la

NOUVELLE

FONDERIE

DE

JACQUES FRANÇOIS ROSART.

DEDIÉE

A SON ALTESSE ROYALE.

Deuxiéme Edition augmentée.

A BRUXELLES,

M D. CC. LXVIII.

still to be admired on the walls of the Foreign Office in Whitehall in London, and he designed a famous biscuit tin and other packages for Huntley & Palmers in Reading.

John Leighton, who also called himself Luke Limner, specialized in the design of publishers' bindings, blocked in gold and colours on cloth; but he also illustrated books, and designed other things such as the Great Exhibition commemoration shield, made in various metals; and both Owen Jones and John Leighton wrote on design – but not explicitly on typographic design.

So we come towards the end of the nineteenth century, when things began to happen which created a situation in the printing industry that made it necessary for 'typographers' to come into existence.

In the early 1880s, photographic line and half-tone blocks were introduced commercially. In 1884 the American Linn Boyd Benton's invention of the punchcutting machine made the Monotype and Linotype composing machines feasible – and then the Benton punchcutting machine mechanized the manufacture of typefaces, making the old laborious hand methods unnecessary. An unlimited number of new typefaces could now be produced, which made specialists in their use inevitable.

These and of course many other inventions in other fields, especially architecture, and the problems of industrialization and mass-production that followed, caused a revolution in thought and design. The Art Workers Guild was founded by Walter Crane and Lewis Day in 1884 – very influential on the Continent, especially in Germany; and in 1891 William Morris and Emery Walker founded the Kelmscott Press, which influenced printing design all over Europe – except France – and in America. But it must not be forgotten that new ideas in typographic design and in the design of books were already active in Britain, and in the USA and on the Continent, before the Kelmscott Press. And what the Kelmscott Press offered was not really new ideas in the design of books:

Title-page of Rosart's *Epreuve des Caractères*, Brussels, 1768, of which Updike says 'There is something pathetic about Rosart's book. It is not very well executed.' In 1749, Jacques-François Rosart, a Belgian punch-cutter and type founder, became the first founder to make movable types for printing music. Original page size of the Epreuve: *c*. 220 × 130 mm.

it was more a reminder of old principles which had been widely ignored; but with one important exception: Morris did bring art – of a kind – back into book pages.

So already well before 1900 we find new ideas in commercial book design: in England, for example, in the work of Dante Gabriel Rossetti, Selwyn Image, Charles Ricketts, and Laurence Housman; in America, Will Bradley and others; and in Germany, Peter Behrens, Otto Eckmann, Otto Hupp, Karl Klingspor, and Walter Tiemann, among other typographic designers, were all active and were all aged over 30 by the year 1900; in Belgium there was Henry Van de Velde, who like Behrens was also an innovating architect. And many others, not forgetting the painters Cézanne, Seurat, Van Gogh, Gauguin, Munch – and sculptors – were all intent on a new vision.

This begins, haltingly, to be reflected in writing about typography, about how to design books. The earliest writers on book design in English were not innovative designers, for example Charles Jacobi in England and Theodore Low de Vinne in America. Jacobi, born in 1853 and at this time Manager of the Chiswick Press, wrote *On the Making and Issuing of Books*, published in 1891, which, in his preface, he says he hopes will be 'of service and value to the author and to all lovers of books' – note that he is not writing for designers. And a year later, in 1892, was published his *Some Notes on Books and Printing*, which went into several editions, subtitled 'A Guide for Authors, Publishers & Others'. Jacobi was a worthy man and a conscientious printer, but not in any sense a creative designer. T. L. de Vinne, born in 1828, also rose from apprenticeship in printing to become proprietor of his own press in New York, the De Vinne Press, and the most eminent printer in America of his day. He was one of the founders of the Grolier Club of New York, and in 1901 that Club published de Vinne's

Of this book, Updike says 'An extremely good specimen of a real modern face roman type was used in Thomas Frognall Dibdin's *Bibliographical Decameron*, printed in 1817 by Bulmer in three volumes. In presswork it is one of the finest of modern volumes. It needed, however, all that the printer could do for it; for its author wrote in an affectedly playful style which makes his books among the most tiresome and irritating in the language.' A page of the *Decameron* is reproduced in Updike's *Printing Types*, vol II, p. 43.

THE

BIBLIOGRAPHICAL

DECAMERON;

OR,

𝕿𝖊𝖓 𝕯𝖆𝖞𝖘 𝕻𝖑𝖊𝖆𝖘𝖆𝖓𝖙 𝕯𝖎𝖘𝖈𝖔𝖚𝖗𝖘𝖊

UPON

ILLUMINATED MANUSCRIPTS,

AND

SUBJECTS CONNECTED WITH

EARLY ENGRAVING, TYPOGRAPHY,

AND BIBLIOGRAPHY.

BY THE

REV. T. F. DIBDIN.

VOL. I.

LONDON:

PRINTED FOR THE AUTHOR, BY W. BULMER AND CO.

𝖘𝖍𝖆𝖐𝖘𝖕𝖊𝖆𝖗𝖊 𝖕𝖗𝖊𝖘𝖘:

AND SOLD BY G. AND W. NICOL, PAYNE AND FOSS, EVANS, JOHN AND
ARTHUR ARCH, TRIPHOOK, AND J. MAJOR.

1817.

THE POETICAL WORKS OF
WILLIAM COWPER
VOLUME III

LONDON

WILLIAM PICKERING

1831

An impeccable title-page designed by the publisher, William Pickering, 1831. Actual size. Note: no punctuation marks used.

THE EMIGRANT,

AND

OTHER POEMS.

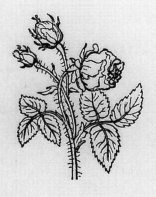

CHISWICK:
PRINTED BY C. WHITTINGHAM.

M DCCC XXXIII.

A less well designed title-page by the printer, Charles Whittingham, 1833, using unnecessary punctuation. Actual size.

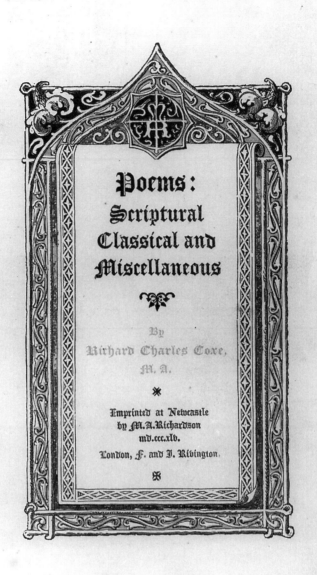

Typographic skill did not exist only in London: a title-page printed in red, green, blue and black in Newcastle upon Tyne, 1845, by a local printer, M. A. Richardson. Page size: 200 × 125 mm.

very handsome book *Title-pages as seen by a Printer* – to which Jacobi contributed an interesting section consisting of 10 different settings, in 10 different styles, of the title-page of his own book *Some Notes on Books and Printing*.

De Vinne's *Title-pages* is a fascinating book, apart from being itself fastidiously and luxuriously printed in various colours. It is the first book I know which studies and illustrates typographic arrangements, in this case of title-pages, historically (de Vinne was a scholar in printing history) as well as critically and aesthetically. De Vinne was no genius, he had 'severe aesthetic limitations' (the distinguished American printer Carl Purington Rollins's words, not mine) but he reflects the conventional good taste of his time. He is perceptive when, in a chapter devoted to Pickering's title-pages, he says 'The Pickering title was not liked in its own time by printers or engravers. Nor is it entirely pleasing to them now. Its simplicity has been condemned as a studied affectation, but the real objection is seldom put forward. A title in the Pickering style is not so easily composed as the ordinary displayed title. To select, group, and arrange the words of a title in a few sizes of roman letter calls for more intelligence and discretion.' How right he was: he is adumbrating the skills of a typographer without using the word. But when he discussed 'off-centre' title-pages, in a chapter called 'The Ragged Title', he reveals a stubborn prejudice. He says 'The ragged title seldom appears in any serious or standard book. Publishers are few who dare to grate the nerves of readers with this eccentricity.' And I have to agree that the examples he illustrates are appalling – but there were also some good ones, which he missed. De Vinne's *Title-pages* was first printed for the Grolier Club of New York in a limited edition of 325 copies, but it was re-issued the next year in a series of four volumes called *The Practice of Typography*. Here again, typography really meant 'Fine Printing' or 'Good Printing'. De Vinne's four volumes, particularly the one called *Plain Printing Types*, were pioneering and of the greatest importance, but they were still, as all previous manuals, addressed to compositors.

De Vinne's books were published in New York and were certainly read in Boston by a man who was a very different kind of printer, Daniel Berkeley Updike. Updike became a printer rather late in life – after he was 30. He became a printer because he was interested in printing and he set up his own business because he was critical of how he saw other people doing it.

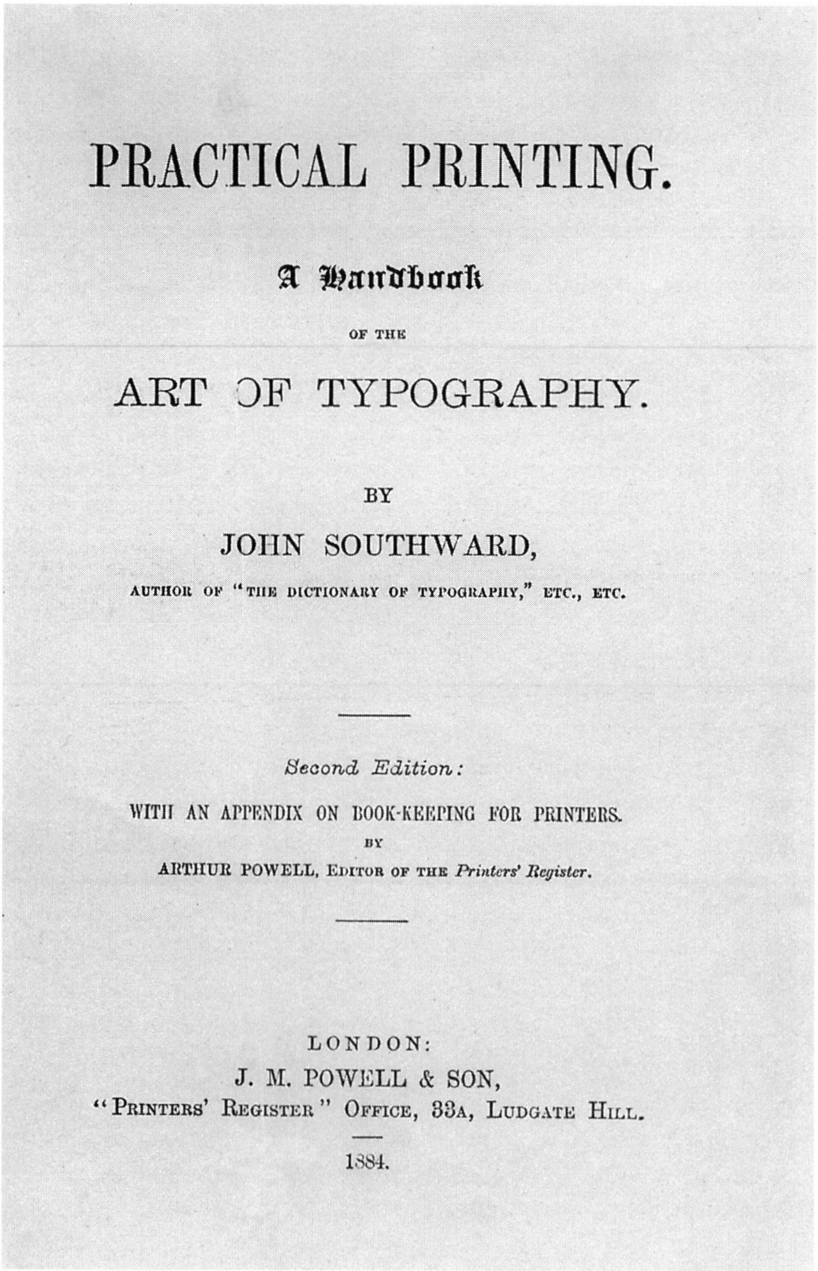

PRACTICAL PRINTING.

𝔄 𝔥𝔞𝔫𝔡𝔟𝔬𝔬𝔨

OF THE

ART OF TYPOGRAPHY.

BY

JOHN SOUTHWARD,

AUTHOR OF "THE DICTIONARY OF TYPOGRAPHY," ETC., ETC.

———

Second Edition:

WITH AN APPENDIX ON BOOK-KEEPING FOR PRINTERS.

BY

ARTHUR POWELL, EDITOR OF THE *Printers' Register.*

———

LONDON:

J. M. POWELL & SON,

"PRINTERS' REGISTER" OFFICE, 33A, LUDGATE HILL.

——

1884.

John Southward (1840–1902) was a Liverpool-born printer-journalist: he was the author of a *Dictionary of Typography*, 1871, which formed the basis of Ringwalt's *American Encyclopaedia of Printing*: and his *Practical Printing*, 1884, shown above, was more about printing than the design of printing. See W. Turner Berry and H. Edmund Poole, *Annals of Printing*, London, 1966.

A page from William Morris's Kelmscott Press edition of *Chaucer*, 1896; one of the last books designed by Morris, in collaboration with Burne-Jones, who wrote 'Chaucer is very much the same sort of person as Morris; unless he can begin his tale at the beginning and go steadily on to the end, he's bothered.' This was the masterpiece of the Kelmscott Press: see *William Morris and the Art of the Book*, Pierpont Morgan Library, New York, 1976. Much reduced.

TYPOGRAPHY

THE PASSAGE from the Written Book to the Printed Book was sudden & complete. Nor is it wonderful that the earliest productions of the printing press are the most beautiful & that the history of its subsequent career is but the history of its decadence. The Printer carried on into Type the tradition of the Calligrapher & of the Calligrapher at his best. As this tradition died out in the distance, the craft of the Printer declined. It is the function of the Calligrapher to revive & restore the craft of the Printer to its original purity of intention & accomplishment. The Printer must at the same time be a Calligrapher, or in touch with him, & there must be in association with the Printing Press a Scriptorium where beautiful writing may be practised and the art of letter-designing kept alive. And there is this further evidence of the dependence of printing upon writing: the great revival in printing which is taking place under our own eyes, is the work of a Printer who before he was a Printer was a Calligrapher & an Illuminator, WILLIAM MORRIS.

❡ The whole duty of Typography, as of Calligraphy, is to communicate to the imagination, without loss by the way, the thought or image intended to be communicated by the Author. And the whole duty of beautiful typography is not to substitute for the beauty or interest of the thing thought and intended to be conveyed by the symbol, a beauty or interest of its own, but, on the one hand, to win access for that communication by the clearness & beauty of the vehicle, and on the other hand, to take advantage of every pause or stage in that communication to interpose some characteristic & restful beauty in its own art. We thus have a reason for the clearness and beauty of the text as a whole, for the especial beauty of the first or

Cover of *The Poster*, May 1900, designed by H. Walmsley. Printed in black, grey, green and brown, with the lettering matching the striking design. Page size: 240 × 170 mm.

Left: A significant passage from T. J. Cobden-Sanderson's *The Ideal Book*, 1900. Type in actual size.

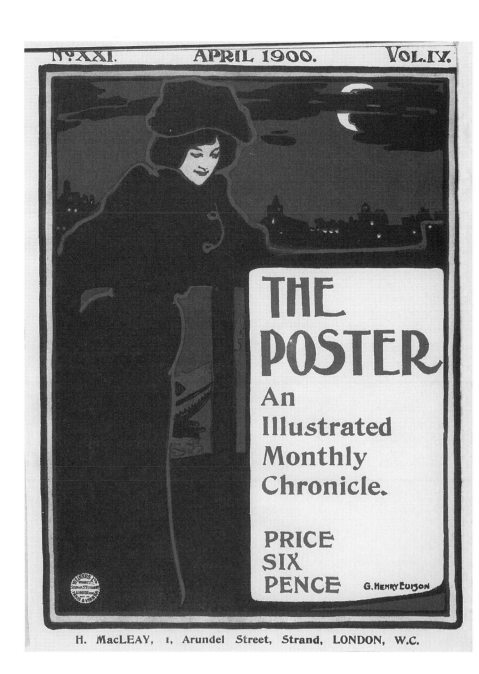

Cover of *The Poster*, April 1900, designed by G. Henry Evison. A vibrant design in red (outline), dark blue, dark brown, and black: the design is more skilful than the lettering. Page size: 240 × 170 mm.

DISPLAY WORK:

THE PRINCIPLES AND
PRACTICE, COMMERCIAL
AND ARTISTIC DISPLAY,
TYPE SELECTION HINTS.

BY

GEORGE JOYNER,

Author of "Fine Printing."

COPYRIGHT.

Printed and Published by
THE RELIANCE PRESS,

6 Broadway,   Southborough,
Lodgate Hill,   Tunbridge Wells,
London, E.C.   Kent.

ARTISTIC
DISPLAY.

III.

PRESENT-DAY display work—except in its strictly commercial or ordinary aspect—cannot be identified with that of a quarter of a century ago. Enterprise and the reproduction by process of the work of both artist and photographer have greatly altered its style during recent years. The tendency of these agencies will be best indicated if I say that the scope of display work has been broadened by the addition of an artistic section.

Modern typefounding enterprise has given the job printer a range in elegant type faces and embellishments that offers him opportunity of making his display tasteful and effective. Process reproduction places at the job printer's disposal the creations of the artist in design, by the proper use of which the former is still further enabled to meet the requirements of modern artistic taste.

There is also a much broader and freer treatment in typographical display generally than existed formerly. Not exactly in fundamental principle, but in manner. Display composition still has one prime object, as we have seen—a message. To present this message in the severest possible manner, by straight lines of varied types, condensed or sprawling as necessitated by the quantity of words, is no longer held to be the best form of typographical display for

Title-page and a text page from Joyner's *Display Work*, c. 1910 with a mention of 'typographical display', and a very peculiar initial opening. Page size: 210 × 145 mm.

29

ALICE'S ADVENTURES IN WON-
DERLAND. BY LEWIS CARROLL
WITH THE ORIGINAL ILLUSTRATIONS
BY JOHN TENNIEL. LONDON: PHILIP
LEE WARNER, PUBLISHER TO
THE MEDICI SOCIETY LD.
VII GRAFTON STREET,
W. MDCCCC
XIV

Title-page of Lewis Carroll's *Alice*, 1914, designed in the Riccardi Press type by Charles T. Jacobi. A very elegant book, but the designer has forced the wording into a shape which disregards the words themselves. Page size: 225 × 157 mm.

His first book, the *Altar Book*, begun in 1893 and published in 1896, was commissioned by a friend, and was designed by Updike very much in the Kelmscott style. It was printed in New York by the De Vinne Press, because Updike at that time did not have the capacity to print such a large book himself. Updike was a new kind of printer: from the very start he worked only for people, or institutions, or firms, who gave him a free hand to design their work in the way he, Updike, thought it ought to be produced, subject of course to basic agreements on style and on costs. Updike's purpose was expressed by him in words which have often been quoted but which can bear repetition: it was 'to make work better for its purpose than was commonly thought worthwhile, and by having one's own establishment, to be free to do so'.

He called his press the Merrymount Press, but merry was not a word commonly used to describe Updike himself. He was not the easiest man in the world to work for: he frequently lost his temper and threw things at his secretary – including even shears – but he certainly had a sense of humour, at least when he was writing: for example: 'What they printed was little to my taste, for there was about their performances a certain conscious pose of the kind that made Lord Minto say at the soulful house-party: "I hate clever people – they're so damned silly".'

In 1911 Updike began giving lectures in Harvard University as part of a course on the Technique of Printing, in the Graduate School of Business Administration. Other lectures in the course were given by William Addison Dwiggins, and in 1915 we know that only two young men registered for the course, although three others – making a total of five – also attended Updike's lectures, given in his office at the Merrymount Press. These lectures ultimately became a great book, *Printing Types, Their History, Forms, and Use* published in two volumes in 1922 – several times reprinted and today available in paperback and still extremely well worth buying. It is an amazing book – with 367 mostly full page illustrations in line, in the first edition – amazing because it is both scholarly and amusing – the first book ever written about printing types and how to use them that was addressed not to the printing trade but to intelligent people interested in printing. And how much better Updike writes about typography than did Stanley Morison: he was more direct, more incisive, more amusing – and he knew more about printing. For example, in his chapter 'On the choice of types':

NOTICE

Mr. D. B. Updike desires to announce that he has this day taken into partnership, in the business of The Merrymount Press, Mr. John Bianchi, who has been connected with the Press since its beginning, in 1893. The style of the firm will be as heretofore, D. B. Updike, The Merrymount Press.

The Merrymount Press, 232 Summer St., Boston
January 1, 1915

An elegant announcement from the Merrymount Press, Boston, in 1915.

Our composing-room has, therefore, only about seven series of standard types for book work, and in all about a score of varieties: 'For what, then,' the reader may ask, 'are all the other types in founders' specimen books?' My answer would be, 'Chiefly to avoid.' If printers had been better educated in their own trade, many of these wretched letters could never have been sold at all. Horace Walpole – who printed none too well at Strawberry Hill – said about people, that nine-tenths of them 'were created to make you want to be with the other tenth.' This is true of types.

At the same time as Updike was beginning to work at his Merrymount Press in Boston, there were many other significant developments in typography and graphic design happening in the United States. There was the extraordinarily talented Will Bradley, who in 1889, aged 21, set up as a freelance designer in Chicago, and whose originality is not, I think, sufficiently appreciated in Britain. There was Frederic Goudy, born in 1865, who in 1899 set up as a freelance designer and designed over one hundred typefaces. Most important of all, and the most relevant to our present purpose, was Bruce Rogers, who became what can be identified as the first respectable international freelance typographer – international, because during the First World War he came to England and advised the Cambridge University Press on its typography – and said some very scathing things about what he found. Rogers started designing trade books and advertisements for the Riverside Press in Cambridge, Mass., in 1896 (then aged 26), and from 1900 to 1912 the Riverside Press allowed him to design a series of limited editions for collectors which made his name as a book designer, and allowed him to set up as a freelance.

To return to Updike: his *Printing Types*, published in 1922, contained over 600 pages of text which were all set by hand – because in Updike's opinion, as also in the opinion of Bernard Newdigate in England, the Linotype and Monotype composing machines could not yet produce as good composition in as good typefaces as a well-trained hand compositor.

But a few years earlier, in London in 1913, a new periodical for printers had appeared, called *The Imprint*, set on the Monotype in a typeface called 'Imprint', the first typeface ever to be specifically designed for machine composition. It was in fact an adaptation of Caslon's Old Face. Caslon's

I. Mr. B.

Q. Mr. B——, will you please tell the committee why you printed this book on card-board?
A. To make it the right thickness. It had to be one inch thick.

— Why that thick, particularly?

— Because otherwise it would not sell. If a book isn't one inch thick it won't sell.

— Do you mean to say that people who buy books select them with the help of a foot rule?

— They have to have some standard of selection.

— So that it is your practice to stretch out the text if it is too short by printing it on egg-box stock?

— Not my practice, particularly. All publishers do it. We are obliged to use this and other means to bring the book up to a proper thickness. You must remember that our prices are not based on the contents of a book but on its size.

— You mention other methods. Would you mind telling us what other methods you use?

— We can expand the letter-press judiciously. We limit the matter to seven words on a page, say, and so get a greater number of pages. We can use large type and can lead considerably.

— But does not that practice hurt the appearance of the page? Make a poor-looking page?

— I am afraid I do not get your meaning.

— I mean to say, is not the page ugly and illegible when you expand the matter to that extent?

— You don't consider the look of a page in making a book. That is a thing that doesn't enter into the production of a book. If I understand you correctly, do you mean to say that it matters how a book looks?

— That was the thought in my mind.

— That's a new idea in book publishing!

type had been designed for printing on hand-made paper, with the knowledge that it would thicken up; but when it was printed on smooth machine-made paper it did not thicken up and looked spidery. Imprint was designed to correct this.

The Imprint magazine, like Updike and his lectures, was a sign of the times. It showed that intelligent men, and even intelligent printers, were beginning to take an interest in how books were designed. It ran for only nine issues; it used the word 'typography' very rarely (once or twice only, I think) in our sense of 'design'. The subject of typographic design is discussed in several places, particularly in no. 5, where a writer, postulating the requirement of the function of the typographer, actually says 'The job cannot be described in a single word'. That word was still not in current use. But this was the periodical that gave Stanley Morison the opportunity to start his career in typography and published his first article; and it is the only serious periodical in the world (as far as I know) that ended its career in mid-sentence – yet another item for congratulation.

The first page of a devastating attack on book design in 1919, written by W. A. Dwiggins and published as a booklet by the so-called 'Society of Calligraphers' (which consisted only of Dwiggins and L. B. Siegfried) in Boston, under the title *Extracts from An Investigation into the Physical Properties of Books as they are at present published*, in an edition undertaken by The Society of Calligraphers.

Up to this point the affair has been pretty much under your control. You have made your individual letter= shapes good according to your lights, and have got them through to metal type. . . . Will they behave decently when they are combined into words? You can't tell yet. *All you can do about this question, in your drawing stage, is to lean hard on the hunches you have picked up as to what letters do to each other when they are fitted together.*

FITTING is the process of working out the ex= actly right amount of space to go between letters.

W. A. Dwiggins writes about letter-fitting, in his own handwriting. From *WAD to RR: A Letter about Designing Type*. Harvard College Library, Cambridge, 1940.

TWO

Germany

We have now to look at the development of typography, as an art and a profession, in Germany.

We will soon be entering the twenty-first century. When we look back to the beginning of the twentieth century, it can be seen that Germany as an industrial nation (and Germany had not been a nation for very long), was already living intellectually in the twentieth century long before we in Britain were doing so; and indeed one wonders how many even influential people in this country are still living in the nineteenth or earlier centuries.

I was lucky enough to go and work in Germany for a few months in the summer of 1936, and for the first time in my life I found and met people, in the Rhineland and in Berlin, who were actually living in, or using, buildings of modern design. It was not uncommon in the Germany I saw, but it was almost unheard of in Britain at that time, and is not very common today.

And when I went to work in a small book-printing firm in Weimar, I was astonished to find that it was a rule for the workmen to wash their hands before touching a sheet of paper – there were washbasins throughout the factory for that purpose. In Germany, people were proud of being printers, a cardinal fact to remember. After all, printing as we know it was invented in the Rhineland; and from the Rhine it was carried all over Europe. Printing is something special in Germany; and so is the legacy of

Albrecht Dürer: drawing and all forms of etching and engraving in black-and-white have remained strong and lively traditions in Germany.

So let us look at the state of affairs in typography in Germany, in – to choose an arbitrary but convenient point – the year 1900. Printing as a trade (and education for that trade) was taken much more seriously in Germany than, I believe, in any other European country. There were great printing schools in Leipzig and Munich and another, important but I think lesser, school in Berlin; and, a very important sign, there were a number of serious and excellent printing trade magazines. To mention only three: *Typographische Mitteilungen, Archiv für Buchdruckerkunst,* which in 1900 became *Archiv für Buchgewerbe und Gebrauchsgraphik;* and *Deutscher Buch- und Steindrucker,* which became the *Deutscher Drucker.* And there were many more, and some very good ones, as the century progressed.

In parenthesis, Germany and Austria also had some outstandingly good art magazines at the turn of the century, e.g. *Pan*, Berlin, 1895–99; *Die Insel*, Leipzig, 1899–1902; *Jugend*, Munich, from 1896; and *Ver Sacrum*, Vienna, 1898–99, which would have certainly been seen by printers and type designers as well as by artists. (See *The Art Press, two centuries of Art Magazines*, edited by Trevor Fawcett & Clive Phillpot, The Art Book Co., London, 1976.)

There were also, in the year 1900 (and increasingly so in the years up to 1914) a number of men designing books and typefaces, whom we might today call typographers – but for whom the title in Germany was 'Buch-kunstler' or 'Schrift-kunstler' – 'Book artist' or 'Type or Lettering Artist'. None of these men, be it noticed, were printers. They included Otto Hupp (a specialist in heraldic design), Walter Tiemann, Otto Eckmann, and Peter Behrens: all were aged over 30 in 1900, and therefore all were older than Bruce Rogers. And in 1900 Karl Klingspor, who had been trained for a career in tobacco, took over control of his family type-founding business, and became the patron of these type designers. He proceeded to commission, art-direct, and manufacture a programme of typefaces which made the Klingspor Type Foundry the most distinguished foundry, artistically speaking, in the world.

The four type designers I have mentioned were followed, in the years up to 1914, by E. R. Weiss, Rudolf Koch, F. W. Kleukens, F. H. Ehmcke, Paul Renner, F. H. Ernst Schneidler, and Hermann Wienck, to name just a

Cover of *Ver Sacrum* (1898–1903): 'The finest Viennese Art Nouveau periodical, and one of the most elegant of all periodicals – the organ of the Vienna Secession'. Anthony Burton in *The Art Press*, Art Book Company, 1976.

Cover of *Jugend* by Otto Eckmann, c. 1896.

Cover of *Jugend*, by Angelo Jank, 1899. 'In 1890 Georg Horth, a member of the
Vienna Secession, founded the Munich magazine *Die Jugend* ('Youth'), which
became a platform for the dissemination of Art Nouveau, giving its name, *Jugendstil*,
to the German movement.' See *Art Nouveau*, ed. Thomas Walters, Academy
Editions, London, 1972.

Cover by Professor Ege for *Archiv für Buchgewerbe*, 1920.

Cover by Hingst for *Archiv für Buchgewerbe*, 1920 (showing the original bleed at foot).

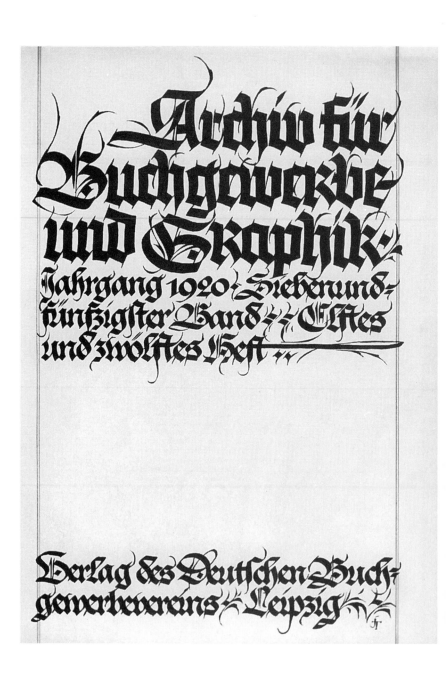

A contrasting cover for *Archiv für Buchgewerbe*, 1920, in pen-drawn calligraphy by Jan Tschichold.

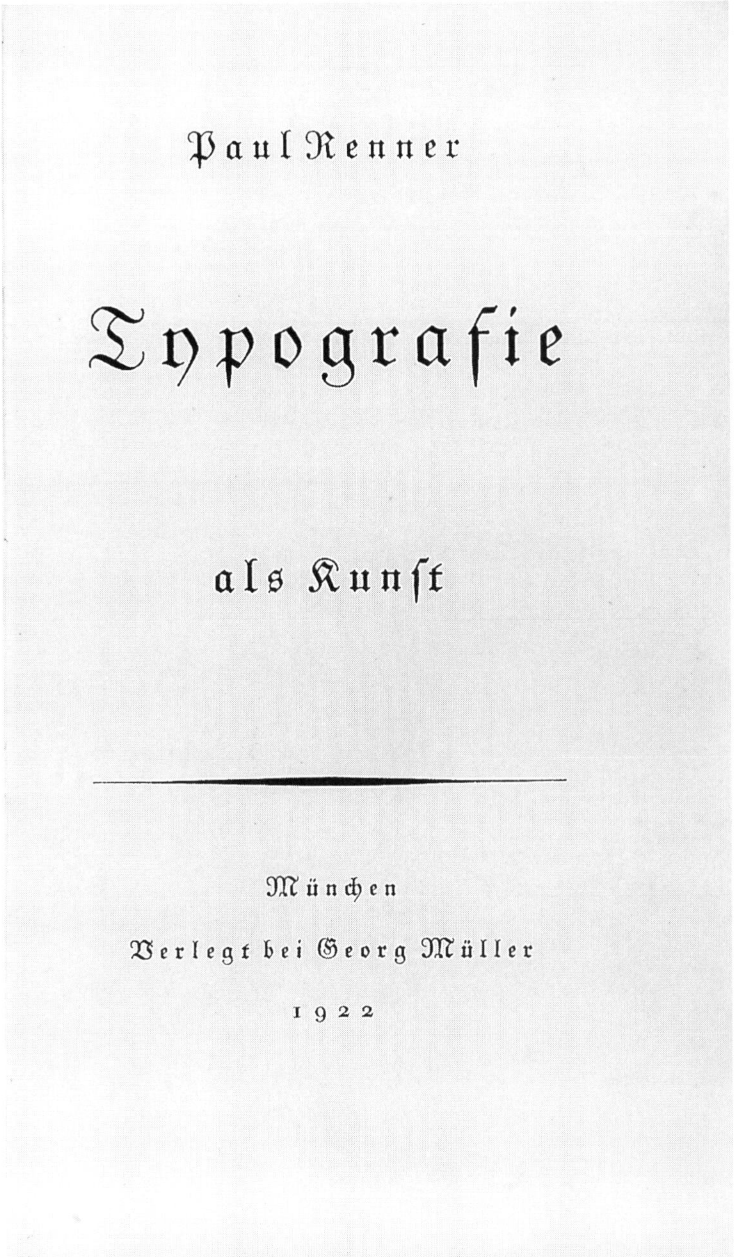

Paul Renner

Typografie

als Kunst

München

Verlegt bei Georg Müller

1922

Title-page of Paul Renner's *Typografie*, Munich, 1922. Probably the first serious book on typography 'as an art' to be published in Europe – but not, like Tschichold's later work, on 'how to do it'.

FUTURA

Although *Futura* is rightly associated with the modernist ideas of the Bauhaus, Paul Renner (1878–1956), graphic designer and teacher, had no Bauhaus affiliation. *Futura*'s many departures from its compass and rule conception reflect a pragmatic functionalism, a deep understanding of history and technique, and a devoted trial and error. The Bauer typefoundry showed the semi-bold in mid 1927, and the light and bold later that year. The family was completed in the 1930s, adapted for Intertype in 1934, and quickly copied by many manufacturers. Bauer's subsidiary, Fundición Tipografica Neufville, took over manufacture and sales in 1972 and continues to sell *Futura* in metal.

Obwohl die *Futura* zu Recht mit den modernistischen Bestrebungen des Bauhauses in Zusammenhang gebracht wird, gehörte Paul Renner, 1878–1956, Graphik Designer und Lehrer nicht zum Bauhaus. Die Schrift besitzt einen geometrischen Formaufbau, dessen pragmatischer Funktionalismus Veränderungen zuläßt. Die *Futura* entstand auf der Basis von Renners Geschichtskenntnis aber auch durch empirisches Vorgehen. Die Bauersche Gießerei zeigte den halbfetten Schnitt Mitte 1927, die magere und die fette Version folgten etwas später im gleichen Jahr. Als Familie war sie 1930 abgeschlossen. 1934 wurde sie von der Intertype für den Zeilenmaschinensatz übernommen und sofort von vielen anderen Gießereien nachgeahmt. Die Fundición Tipográfica Neufville, S.A., früher eine Tochtergesellschaft von Bauer, betreibt seit 1972 die Fertigung und den Verkauf der *Futura* als Bleisatzschrift.

Fundición Tipográfica Neufville S.A.   Paul Renner

a b c d e f **g** h i j k l m n o p q r s t u v w x y z
A B C D E F **G** H I J K L M N O P Q R S T U V W X Y Z
1 2 3 4 5 6 7 8 9 0 fi fl ß &

Futura évoque à juste titre le radicalisme du Bauhaus. Pourtant, Paul Renner (1878–1956) n'a jamais fait partie du Bauhaus. Il était graphiste et enseignait à l'école d'imprimerie de Munich. Le *Futura* se voulait géométrique. Mais le fonctionnalisme de Renner s'est très pragmatiquement plié à bien des corrections. Il travaillait d'instinct en puisant dans ses vastes connaissances historiques et techniques. La fonderie Bauer publia d'abord le demi-gras, vers la mi-1927. Le maigre et le gras suivirent, la même année. La famille fut complétée au cours des années 1930. Intertype l'adopta en 1934. Puis vinrent toutes sortes de copies. La Fundición Tipográfica Neufville, S.A., une filiale de Bauer, reprit l'affaire en 1972 et vend encore le *Futura* en mobile.

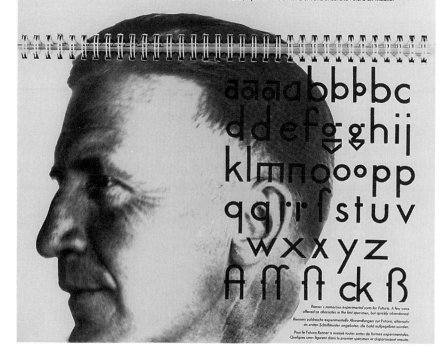

Renner's numerous experimental sorts for Futura. A few were offered as alternates in the first specimen, but quickly abandoned

Renners zahlreiche experimentelle Abwandlungen zur Futura, alternativ im ersten Schriftmuster angeboten, die bald aufgegeben wurden.

Pour le Futura Renner a essayé toutes sortes de formes expérimentales. Quelques unes figurent dans le premier spécimen et disparaissent ensuite.

A heavily reduced opening from *26 Letters*, designed by Banks and Miles, published by ATypI in 1989, showing Paul Renner and his famous typeface Futura. Original printed in red and black on pale green.

few. The Studio Special Number on *The Art of the Book*, published in 1914, shows that no less than eleven of the German and Austrian designers illustrated were called 'Professor'. The title of 'Professor' in Germany may mean only that the person so named was a teacher somewhere, but it does indicate if nothing else the respect with which these designers were regarded in their own country.

We had no 'professors' of Graphic Art or Typography in Britain at that time; but apart from the architect W. R. Lethaby, Professor of Architecture at the Central School, and later at the Royal College of Art, we had Emery Walker (we did at least give him a knighthood, but he had to wait some time for it), Edward Johnston, Eric Gill, and J. H. Mason – all of whom were invited, at various times before 1914, to go to Germany, and indeed went, to offer their skills to German private presses and commercial publishers, who seem to have appreciated them more than the people in their own country of England.

We said that Germany was into the twentieth century, at least intellectually, before we were. Professor Pevsner was very interesting on this subject in *Academies of Art Past and Present*, published by Cambridge University Press in 1940. He points out, first, that Germany was ahead of other countries in appointing *designers* – not artists – as heads of Art Schools: for example Behrens at Düsseldorf and Poelzig at Breslau, both in 1903; the Dutchman Van de Velde at Weimar in 1902; and Bruno Paul at Berlin in 1907. These appointments were all the result of a seven-year visit to Britain by Hermann Muthesius, an architect, who was sent to Britain as special attaché to the German Embassy to study English housing, and who on his return to Germany was appointed Inspector of the Schools of Arts and Crafts in the Prussian Board of Trade.

How the ideas of Ruskin, William Morris, and the British Arts and Crafts Movement did (and did not) influence the reform of art education in Germany is a complicated story: Pevsner indicates that while our ideas for the reform of art education ran out of steam around 1900, they went from strength to strength in Germany: he writes: 'The British organisation about 1900 was – generally speaking – an outcome of two unrelated lines of development, that of the nineteenth century art school, and that of the Arts and Crafts Movement; Germany's endeavours at the same time were directed by men who knew that architecture and design would be more

Peter Behrens, 1868–1940, designer.

Fritz Helmut Ehmcke, 1878–1965.
Author of *Die historische Entwicklung der abendländischen Schriftformen* (The historical development of Western type forms).

Walter Tiemann, 1876–1951, Leipzig, type designer. Tschichold became his special student at Leipzig Academy when Tiemann appointed him assistant in charge of evening classes in lettering, in 1921.

Heinrich Wieynck, Dresden, an early typography teacher of Tschichold.

essential to a genuine style of the twentieth century than painting and sculpture, and who acted accordingly.'

The career of Peter Behrens is particularly relevant here. He was born in 1868 in Hamburg, and began his working life as a painter – in the art nouveau or 'Jugendstil' mode. But very soon he was designing rooms, houses, furniture, teapots, typefaces, catalogues, books, the lot. In 1907 he became design adviser to the great electrical engineering firm of AEG in Berlin – perhaps the first industrial design appointment ever made – and it is his work for them, and indeed for other great German firms like Mannesmann, that shows how Germany was into the twentieth century long before we were. Behrens is an extraordinary figure. He is known, most of all, as an architect: the turbine factory he designed for AEG in 1909 is illustrated in Pevsner's *Pioneers of Modern Design* and Pevsner says of it 'Here for the first time the imaginative possibilities of industrial architecture were visualized' – and it is still standing in Berlin. But Behrens was never a qualified architect: he was entirely self-taught. Let Kurt Rowland have the last word on Behrens as an architect. In Rowland's valuable *History of the Modern Movement*, he says 'Behrens' importance lies as much in the fact that he was teacher to three of the most influential form-givers of the modern world: Walter Gropius, Ludwig Mies van der Rohe, and Le Corbusier' – quite a group of young men to have had working on one's staff.

When Behrens came to designing type – and he did this very seriously and systematically, and provided several types with whole ranges of ornaments to go with them – he was faced by the problem that bothered every other type designer and lettering artist: the fact that the Germans had never abandoned the black-letter or gothic, but continued to use it as their normal type, while also admitting the existence of both roman type and sans serif.

Behrens, and nearly all the other type designers mentioned, designed both black-letter and roman types, and also searched for a type that would provide a compromise between the two. We will look at some examples; and before we rush to condemn them – because some look very strange to us – we should try not to judge them harshly until we have acquired a much deeper knowledge of German art and culture than most of us have had the opportunity to acquire.

Stanley Morison, in *Type Designs of the Past and Present*, published in

tatem temporum non audent. Ita fit ut adsint propterea quod officium sequuntur, taceant autem idcirco quia periculum vitant. Quid ergo? audacissimus ego ex omnibus? Minime. An tanto officiosior quam ceteri? Ne istius quidem laudis ita

Peter Behrens' Antiqua typeface, 1908.

BUCHHANDLUNG
Handſchriften
des 13. und 16. Jahrhunderts

MDCCXL
Friedrich der Große

Peter Behrens' Mediäval typeface, 1914.

Meine Beichte!
2 Leo Tolstoi 4
Antike Kunst

Behrens' Schrift, 1902.

Behrens' Kursiv, 1907.

Behrens was one of Germany's leading type designers who was faced by the problem of black-letter or gothic, which Germany had never abandoned, versus roman type which continued to be viewed in Germany as a 'foreign' type.

1926, wrote 'A number of the new German roman types are excessively modern and painful, witness the Eckmann...' and in his Review of *Recent Typography in England, the United States, France and Germany*, published in 1927, he wrote 'Most of the credit for the notable improvement in German type design is due to Dr Karl Klingspor's enterprise and sagacity' – Klingspor's first attempt, the *Eckmann-Schrift* (1901) was not happy, nor indeed is there much to be said for the first type to be designed by the architect Peter Behrens and cut in 1902. But Morison added, a few lines later, 'Klingspor's recent antiquas [i.e. roman types] also include a highly successful character designed by Peter Behrens in 1914'. What Updike said, both about German types and Morison's opinions of them, is another matter.

Morison was, in fact, not very sympathetic to experiments or the new in either art or architecture. The printer in Germany of whom Morison did approve was Carl Ernst Poeschel (born 1874) who had spent some time first in America, then in England with Cobden-Sanderson and Morris, before returning to Germany to join the family printing business of Poeschel & Trepte in Leipzig. Poeschel was a great printer and also a publisher, who with Anton Kippenberg took over control of Insel Verlag in Leipzig in 1905, when it was on the point of failing, and made it into the great publishing house it soon became. Poeschel & Trepte were the printers of many of those superb little Insel Verlag colour plate books that became, in Allen Lane's day, the models for the King Penguins – a collection of which has been presented to the Morison Room in Cambridge by Hans and Tanya Schmoller. At a time when German design was heavily and extravagantly under the influence of art nouveau, the 'Jugendstil', Poeschel showed German book designers the way back to sanity and simplicity – and in our pursuit of typography as a career, we may note that we learn from Hans Schmoller's article on Poeschel in *Signature* magazine that Poeschel held courses in typographical design in Hamburg and Leipzig in 1903 and 1904 – and that in 1907 Poeschel and Walter Tiemann founded the first German private press, the Janus-Presse.

Poeschel, important as he was, probably did not have much influence on German printing; he may have had more in England. He had, for example, a strong influence on the early work of Oliver Simon at the Curwen Press.

*

ARCHIV
FÜR
BUCHGEWERBE
UND GRAPHIK

JAHRGANG 1920

BAND 57

HEFT

1/2

*

AFBUG

*

VERLAG

DES DEUTSCHEN

BUCHGEWERBEVEREINS

LEIPZIG

*

A 1920 title-page designed by Carl Ernst Poeschel, who had spent some time in America, and then in England, before returning to Germany to join the family printing business of Poeschel & Trepte in Leipzig.

We come now to the crisis in our story of typography and design in Germany, the appearance of that remarkable school, the Bauhaus, in Weimar and 'die neue Typographie' – the so-called 'New Typography'.

As our limited purpose is to detect the emergence of the professional typographer, I have to say that in my opinion the first man who most fully earned that title in Germany, the first man who in any country performed all the functions of a modern typographer, was Jan Tschichold. The so-called 'modern movement' was not only a European phenomenon, it was very much a German movement. In Berlin, in 1920, for example, were to be found working, among many others, the Dadaists Kurt Schwitters and John Heartfield, who invented photomontage; the Russians El Lissitzky, Gabo, and Archipenko; the Hungarians Moholy-Nagy and Peri, the Dutch architects Oud, Van Essteren and Van Doesburg – and many others, including Swedes, Danes, and Italians.

For some years before that, the Italian Futurists, the Russian Constructivists, the Dadaists in Zurich and Paris, De Stijl in Holland, had all used typography to demonstrate their ideas, not so much in words but in images. The printing industry, all over Europe, and in America, was, in terms of design – and functional utility – extremely backward. As Herbert Spencer (our first Professor of Typography, created in 1978) wrote: 'Painters, writers, poets, architects and others came to printing from outside the industry, bursting with ideas and exhilarated by a new concept of art and society, determined to make their voices heard effectively, and they seized upon printing because they recognized it for what it properly is – a potent means of conveying ideas and information – and not for what much of it had then become – a kind of decorative art remote from the realities of contemporary society.' Those men in Europe at the end of the terrible First World War demanded and needed change; in Britain after the war, the same thing did not happen, at least in any revolutionary way; and also I think that it can be said that the *Imprint* group (and after the war men like Harold Curwen and his artists, and later on Eric Gregory and Eric Humphries at Lund Humphries) were, in a small way, relating the printing industry to the realities of contemporary society – which was no doubt one reason why most of us in Britain turned a blind eye to the Modern Movement.

To go back to the Bauhaus at Weimar. Tschichold was never a student or a teacher at the Bauhaus, but he went as a young printing student, aged

ABONNEMENT BIJ VOORUITBETALING BINNENLAND 4.50 BUITENLAND 5.50 PER JAARGANG. VOOR ANNONCES WENDE MEN ZICH TOT DEN UITGEVER.

MAANDBLAD VOOR DE BEELDENDE VAKKEN. REDACTIE THEO VAN DOESBURG. UITGAVE X. HARMS TIEPEN.

ADRES VAN REDACTIE: KORT GALGEWATER 3 LEIDEN. ADMINISTRATIE: X. HARMS TIEPEN, HYPOLITUSBUURT 37 DELFT, INTERC. TEL. 729 EN 690.

1e JAARGANG.   APRIL   NEGENTIENHONDERDACHTTIEN.   NUMMER 6.

Cover and title lettering of *De Stijl*, founded and designed by Theo van Doesburg, 1917. See H. Spencer, *Pioneers of Modern Typography*, 2nd edn., 1982, pp 86–91.

21, to the first Bauhaus Exhibition at Weimar in August 1923, and there for the first time he actually saw what he had already heard about, but never yet seen: examples of the Modern Movement in art. And he was intoxicated by them. So, I may be allowed to say, was I, at about the same age, when I saw the first examples of Tschichold's own asymmetric typography which I found on my desk when I went to work at Lund Humphries at Bradford in June 1939. I had previously seen beautiful typography, shown me by Bernard Newdigate and others, but these few examples of Tschichold's work were positively exciting, new, and elegant. The typography of the Bauhaus was never elegant: strident, even compelling, yes: but never elegant.

So the young Tschichold, brought up in an ordinary, humble, working-class family in Leipzig – Biedermeier furniture and possibly some art nouveau ornaments – his father was a sign-writer, so lettering lay about him in his infancy – first saw modern art when he was 21. Two years later, when he was only 23, his first manifesto was published in a special number of the German printing trade journal *Typographische Mitteilungen* – the official magazine of the Printing Trades Union, which Bertram Evans says 'had a circulation of 22,000 copies entirely among working compositors'. This was the first time that anyone had tried to explain the New Typography to printers, and Tschichold told them not only how to do it but also that they *should* do it: one of the messages being 'You must now, to be contemporary, use sans serif type, and not black-letter'. This message was in fact printed in roman type, perhaps because the printers of the journal did not have a sans serif text face!

What in fact was the New Typography?

A lot of heavy weather has been made out of the New Typography, especially in the USA and in Britain, where few people understood it and fewer accepted it, because the words meant, and often still mean, entirely different things to different people.

Typography can be said to be merely 'using type'. So any use of type is typography: in that sense, the work of the Positivists and the Constructivists and the Suprematists and all the other extrematists was the New Typography, and all that most people saw was big black type, rules and circles and squares and triangles used in every unconventional and startling way. So ordinary people, particularly in Britain and America,

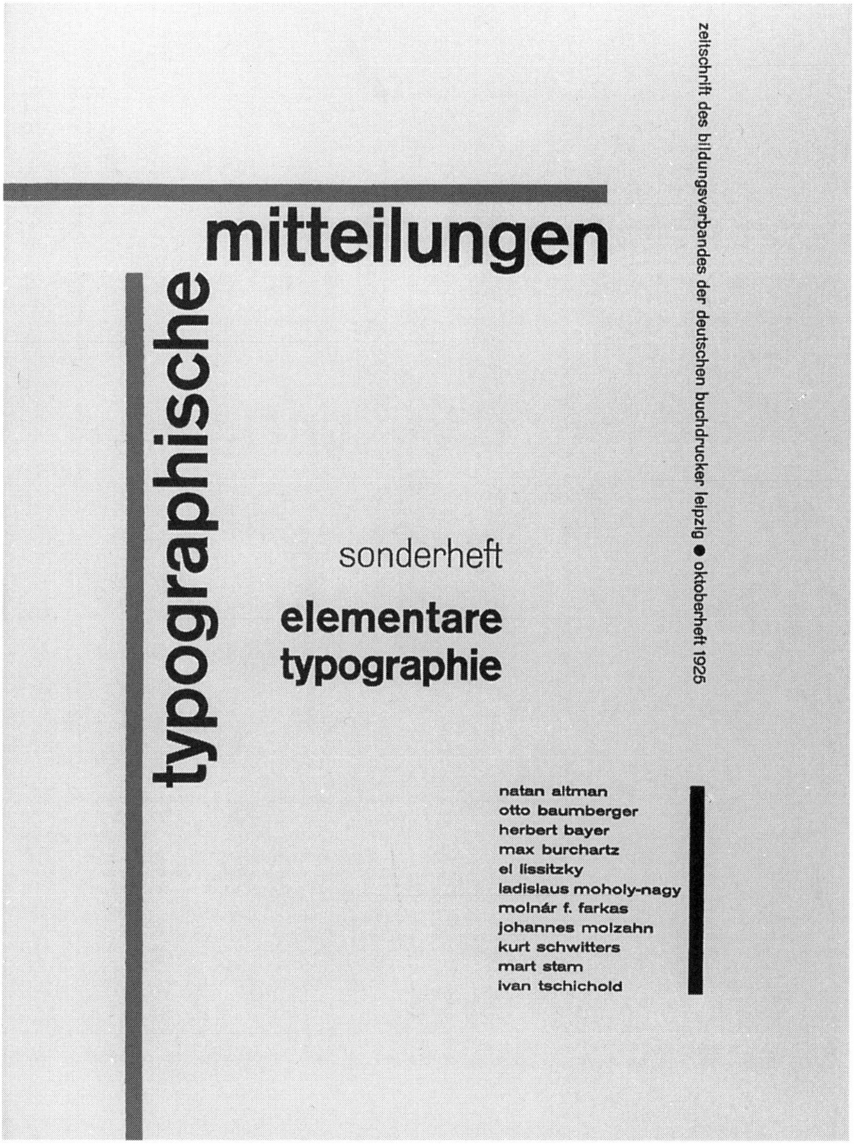

mitteilungen

typographische

zeitschrift des bildungsverbandes der deutschen buchdrucker leipzig ● oktoberheft 1925

sonderheft

elementare
typographie

natan altman
otto baumberger
herbert bayer
max burchartz
el lissitzky
ladislaus moholy-nagy
molnár f. farkas
johannes molzahn
kurt schwitters
mart stam
ivan tschichold

Title-page of the first publication on the 'new typography': Tschichold's article
'elementare typographie' issued as a special number of the Leipzig printing periodical
Typographische Mitteilungen ('Typographic News'), October 1925. Note list of
contributors on right, including 'ivan' tschichold. Printed in red and black. Reduced.

Die Typographie Gutenbergs, die bis fast in unsre Tage reicht, bewegt sich in ausschliesslich linearen Dimensionen. Durch die Einschaltung des photographischen Verfahrens erweitert sie sich zu einer neuen Typographie mit neuer, heute als total bekannter Dimensionalität. Die Anfangsarbeiten dazu wurden von den illustrierten Zeitungen, Plakaten, Akzidenzdrucken schon geleistet.

Bis vor kurzem hielt man krampfhaft fest an einem Setzmaterial und einer Satztechnik, die zwar die Reinheit des Linearen gewährleisteten, das neue Tempo des Lebens aber ausser acht lassen mussten. Erst in der allerletzten Zeit hat eine typographische Arbeit eingesetzt, die durch eine kontrastreiche Verwendung von typographischem Material (Buchstaben, Zeichen) den Zusammenhang mit dem heutigen Leben zu schaffen versuchte.

Die bisherige Starre der typographischen Praxis wurde aber durch diese Bemühungen kaum gelockert. Eine wirksame Lockerung kann nur bei weitestgehender, umfassender Verwendung der photographisch-zinkographisch-galvanoplastischen und ähnlichen Techniken erreicht werden. Die Biegsamkeit, Beweglichkeit dieser Techniken bringt Ökonomie und Schönheit in eine neue Wechselbeziehung. Mit der Entwicklung der Bildtelegraphie, die die Beschaffung von vollendet genauen Illustrationen im Augenblick ermöglicht, wird es wahrscheinlich dazu kommen, dass auch philosophische Werke mit den gleichen Mitteln arbeiten werden — wenn auch auf höherer Ebene — wie jetzt die

A design by El Lissitzky in 'elementare typographie'.

58

Die alte Kunst schuf Bilder, um die Räume zu schmücken, in denen man sie ungestört betrachtete. Diese Bilder stellen die Psychologie des geniessenden Bürgers dar. Die neue Kunst war durch die Auswahl ihrer Materialien (Stahl, Gips, Glas usw.) gezwungen, zu einer gleichsam mechanischen Technik, ähnlich der industriellen Technik, zu gelangen. DIE NEUE KUNST SCHAFFT NICHT BILDER, SONDERN GEGENSTÄNDE, materielle Objekte. Sie entspringt der Psychologie des Werktätigen, des Proletariers ●

Herbert Bayer: Typosignet für einen Glasmaler

ZU DEN
AUFSÄTZEN UND BEISPIELEN

Das vorliegende Heft war ursprünglich als Bauhausheft gedacht. Das Bauhaus ist aber nur *ein* Stützpunkt der Kampflinie für die Neue Kultur. Die Ideen, für die das Bauhaus in Dessau (früher Weimar) eintritt, werden außer vom Bauhaus noch von einer ganzen Reihe nicht dem Bauhaus angehörender Künstler, Wissenschaftler, Techniker auf der ganzen Welt, bis jetzt hauptsächlich in Europa und Amerika, verfochten. Daher war es notwendig, daß sich das geplante Heft nicht auf die schon im BAUHAUSE geleistete typographische Arbeit beschränkte, sondern die Arbeit in ALLEN Ländern, die auf diesem Gebiet Vertreter aufzuweisen haben, berücksichtigte. Vor allem ist Rußland hier zu nennen, dessen Vertreter El Lissitzky, Typ des neuen Gestalters, zu den besten Vertretern der Neuen Typographie zählt. Schließlich sollte der irreführende und von Mitläufern in Verruf gebrachte Name »Konstruktivismus« vermieden werden. Alle diese Erwägungen führten am Ende zur Wahl des Titels »Elementare Typographie«, der auch den Sinn unsrer Arbeit wirklich trifft. Zu den Aufsätzen ist kurz zu bemerken, daß die Artikel »Programm der Konstruktivisten« und »Elementare Gesichtspunkte« von Altman, vom Herausgeber bearbeitet sind. Zum Teil enthielten die Originale viele Fremdwörter, die eine Bearbeitung für deutsche Leser notwendig machten (Altman), zum Teil mußte der Aufbau abgeändert werden (Programm der Konstruktivisten). *Altman* gehört zu den besten Vertretern der neuen russischen Kunst. Er betätigte sich nicht allein auf den Gebieten der Malerei und Plastik, sondern auch mit großem Erfolg auf denen der Bühnenkonstruktion und der dekorativen Architektonik von Meetings in Moskau. *Moholy-*

Nagy ist Meister am Dessauer Bauhaus. Er entstammt der ungarischen Aktivisten-Gruppe Ma (=Heute).
Den meisten Lesern wird vielleicht nicht alles in diesem Heft Gezeigte ohne Erklärung verständlich sein. Darum sei im nachstehenden versucht, kurze Erläuterungen zu den einzelnen Arbeiten zu geben. – Eine exakte Aufeinanderfolge der Arbeiten des einzelnen Künstlers und entsprechend manchen Artikeln war aus technischen Gründen leider nicht völlig durchzuführen.
Auf Seite **193** ist ein Typosignet von *Kurt Schwitters* (aus dem Merz-Heft Ty-Re) gezeigt. Ein Typosignet ist ein Signet, das sich ohne Mühe mit rein typographischen, in jeder Druckerei vorhandenen Mitteln nachsetzen, verkleinern und vergrößern läßt. (Ein andres Typosignet, von Herbert Bayer, befindet sich auf dieser Seite.) Für einen schöpferisch veranlagten Setzer bieten sich auf diesem Felde große Möglichkeiten. Es folgen einige Arbeiten von *El Lissitzky*, der als Führer der Neuen Typographie an den Anfang des Heftes gestellt ist. Auf den Seiten **194** und **195** befinden sich die Abbildungen der Mär von zwei Quadraten; eine Übersetzung hiervon ist oben auf Seite 191 gegeben. In diesem Buche entspricht Stellung und Formwert des einzelnen Buchstabens und des Wortes den Zug- und

Johannes Molzahn 1923: Postkarte

212

Designs by Herbert Bayer, above, and Johannes Molzahn, below, in 'elementare typographie'.

The
NEW TYPOGRAPHY
& MODERN LAYOUTS

by

Frederic Ehrlich.

Instructor in typographic
Layout & Design at the N. Y.
Printers Ass'n. Mechanics
Institute & formerly in charge
of the Advertising & Layout
classes at Cooper Union.

Title-page of Frederic Ehrlich's attempt to teach the New Typography, New York,
1932: serious and possibly useful to some, but faulty.

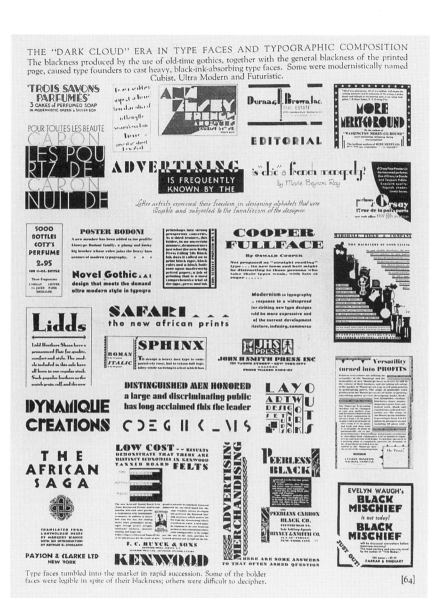

THE "DARK CLOUD" ERA IN TYPE FACES AND TYPOGRAPHIC COMPOSITION
The blackness produced by the use of old-time gothics, together with the general blackness of the printed page, caused type founders to cast heavy, black-ink-absorbing type faces. Some were modernistically named Cubist, Ultra Modern and Futuristic.

Type faces tumbled into the market in rapid succession. Some of the bolder faces were legible in spite of their blackness; others were difficult to decipher.

[64]

Another page from Ehrlich's *The New Typography*: typefaces tumbled into the market!

Reproductions of magazine pages that illustrate the results obtained when the agencies directed their efforts toward a solution of the underlying principles of the New Typography. Basic balances were beginning to function.

The above compositions show how admirably the new balances function even when traditional faces are used.

The printed specimens show marked influences of the "New Note" in advertising layouts and the peace and calm that followed the tempestuous voyage of the pseudo-modernism of a previous period.

[94]

Page 94 in Ehrlich's *The New Typography*. He says 'The printed specimens show marked influences of the "New Note" in advertising layouts and the peace and calm that followed the tempestuous voyage of the pseudo-modernism of a previous period.' I wonder.

ERASMUS VON ROTTERDAM

DAS LOB DER
TORHEIT

Übersetzt von Alfred Hartmann
Mit den Holbeinischen Randzeichnungen
herausgegeben von Emil Major

M.CM.XL.IV

VERLAG BIRKHÄUSER
BASEL

When Tschichold moved from Germany to Switzerland, he returned to traditional centred typography, as being more suitable for the books he was now designing. Title-page of *Das Lob der Torheit* ('In Praise of Folly'), by Erasmus, published by Birkhäuser in Basel, 1944. Printed in black and red, actual size.

THOMAS MORE
· UTOPIA ·
Aus dem Lateinischen
übersetzt von Alfred
Hartmann

BASEL · MCMXLVII
IM VERLAG BIRKHÄUSER

Another Tschichold title-page for Birkhäuser, 1947. Actual size.

thought that was all there was to it: type upside down or at 45° , with a lot of black and red heavy rules thrown in. But that was not the real New Typography. El Lissitzky and Herbert Bayer, and Doesberg and Schwitters were not naive idiots. Their wilder designs were attempts to create images and emotional sensations rather than sentences to be read.

When Tschichold wrote about the New Typography, he meant, by typography, communication: the communication of words. For him, as for Stanley Morison and Beatrice Warde, typography was the servant art, by which an author's words were communicated to his readers.

Tschichold, before he ever saw the Bauhaus Exhibition, was already a highly talented young calligrapher, both traditional and experimental, and also an artist and craftsman of great skill. When he visited the Bauhaus, he saw abstract art and saw how exciting it could be – and he saw typographical material used in an abstract way. He saw too, very quickly, as few others did, how these ideas and methods could be used to revive and re-energise day-to-day printing. Asymmetric typography – asymmetry was a keynote in the New Typography – is merely an alternative to symmetrical or traditional typography. Tschichold was already an excellent traditional designer before he sounded the trumpet of asymmetry.

After some years practising and propagandising for the New Typography, Tschichold was honoured to be counted among those artists accused by the Nazis of 'Kultur-bolshevismus': after all, he did at one time sign his work 'Ivan Tschichold'. He was put in prison, had his official teaching post taken away from him, and was then allowed to leave the country – he was not a Jew – and emigrate to Switzerland with his wife and son. In order to earn his living among the Swiss, he found that he had to revert to traditional typography, quite apart from the fact that asymmetric typography, which is nervous, in tension, the opposite of static, is not an appropriate style for many kinds of book.

Tschichold's 'New Typography' was not, perhaps, so revolutionary as Tschichold himself proclaimed it to be. It was also called 'functional typography' – but all good typography is functional typography – it has to be. Tschichold's *Neue Typographie* was an alternative style, not a different function. The New Typography got a bad name because people did not understand it, any more than they understood abstract art: it offended them and shocked them – as it was sometimes intended to do – and they did not bother to look long enough at Tschichold's work to see what he was actually doing.

A few people in England did, however. The Bradford printers Lund Humphries, at the suggestion of the American designer McKnight Kauffer, then working in London, gave him an exhibition in their London office in 1935. And the Double Crown Club invited Tschichold to dinner and to address the Club in London in April 1937. The menu specially designed for the dinner reveals that the designer of the menu, a printer-member, and (I suspect) the President and most of the rest of the club, had not got a clue as to what the New Typography was about.

And in 1934 a book was published in America and in Britain called *The New Typography & Modern Layouts*, written by the instructor in Typographical Design at the New York Mechanics Institute, one Frederic Ehrlich. It makes the same point as the Double Crown Club menu. I am amazed that it was ever published, and I quake to think how many copies were sold (see p.60).

From the 1930s, Tschichold was both practising typography – that was how he earned his daily bread – and writing about it. It is significant, apropos to our search for the emergence of the professional typographer, that up to and during the Second World War he was writing for the printing trade, chiefly in Germany and Switzerland. His instructional books were the first systematic, sensible, and truly efficient books on the subject ever written, and they were addressed to compositors. He wrote one book – not really a book, but a 24-page A4 booklet – on how to draw layouts, in 1932. He showed in this booklet how a designer can draw his layout for a title-page or a letter-head, or whatever, by tracing from type specimens in pencil, and create what is as good as a proof without incurring the expense of a proof; Thibaudeau had done this in his *Manuel Français de Typographie Moderne* in 1924, but in an expensive and elaborate format that few compositors could have afforded or would even have seen. Shades of Francis Meynell, and sometimes Morison and Oliver Simon, with their numerous trial proofs of title-pages. They were all perfectionists, but Tschichold was the more practical typographer.

It was a fitting and triumphant climax of his career when in 1946 he was invited by Allen Lane, on Oliver Simon's advice, to come to England and take charge of all Penguin Books typography. That was the perfect example of what the new profession of typography could lead to. Such a job could not, I believe, have been undertaken in Britain with the same success at any earlier time. Tschichold himself summed up the matter in an article written in 1948, while he was still working in England. He wrote: 'Alle Kunst des Satzes hat die auf langer Erfahrung fussenden Erkentnisse uber die beste Leserlichkeit und handwerklich sinnvollen Aufbau zu beachten. Beides ist von Tagesmoden und politischen Auffassungen unabhängig. Es kann daher weder eine eigentliche "neue" noch eine "reaktionare" Typographie geben, sondern nur guten oder schlechten Satz'. 'The art of setting type is always concerned with how to achieve maximum legibility by the most technically efficient means. These aims have nothing to do with either fashion or politics. There can therefore be neither a genuinely new, nor a 'reactionary' typography, but only either good or bad setting.' And to avoid giving the impression that the New Typography and the work of Tschichold was totally misunderstood in the United States, here is something written by Paul Rand, an American designer who certainly understood what Tschichold was about. He wrote, at the end of an article called 'The good old Neue Typographie' in 1959: 'Good typography, American or otherwise, is not a question of nationality, but of practicality; namely, it is that of resolving the specific problem in adequate formal terms. In the early twenties, when Tschichold wrote his revolutionary book on modern typography he did not call it German or Swiss or French, he called it simply 'Die neue Typografie'.

Ex Libris, about 1925, in
black and red. Actual size.

LA FRANCE FLORISSANTE.

LA France, en paix avec tous ſes voiſins, joüiſſoit des avantages que les ſoins & les travaux du Roy luy avoient procurez. Auſſi reſpectée au dehors, que calme au dedans, elle voyoit la Juſtice, la Religion, & l'Abondance régner par la ſageſſe du Prince ; & les Sciences, & les Arts fleurir par ſa magnificence, & ſes libéralitez.

C'eſt le ſujet de cette Médaille. Le Roy eſt repréſenté ſous la figure d'Apollon, Dieu des beaux Arts. La branche d'Olive, & la Corne d'a-bondance, qu'il tient en ſes mains, ſont les ſymboles du bonheur ; & de la paix. Les mots de la Légende, FELICITAS TEMPORUM, ſigni-fient, *la félicité du régne.* L'Exergue marque la date *1663.*

The 'Romain du Roi' typeface, cut by P. Grandjean, 1702. See p. 71. Original page size: 432 × 292 mm.

THREE

France

Having looked at the origins and progress of typography as a profession in Britain, America and Germany, we turn to France, where we find something completely different.

The British private press movement, starting with William Morris, which had such a profound influence in Europe and the United States, was noticed in France, but it was not copied. The path taken by the French in typography after William Morris was so oblivious of what we and the Germans and the Americans were doing, so completely in contradiction to what we were admiring, that we have to remind ourselves that the French do have a great – a staggeringly great – tradition of typographic design. France was the country of Garamond, Granjon, Le Bé, Tory, the Estiennes, de Colines, Jean de Tournes, and so on; French typography and French typefaces were once the best in Europe and an inspiration for all time, not least to Francis Meynell and Stanley Morison in their early days at the Pelican Press in London.

And during the seventeenth and eighteenth centuries, France continued to make enormous contributions to world typography.

Cardinal Richelieu had his own private press, and in the middle of the seventeenth century persuaded Louis Treize to found the Imprimerie Royale in the Louvre, which became a continuing and important influence on French printing; at the end of the century, Louis Quatorze ordered a

vrage le plus utile qu'il fera poffible ; mais comme je n'ofe efpérer malgré cela d'atteindre le point de perfection auquel je defire de porter l'Art Typographique, je profiterai avec plaifir des critiques honnêtes &éclairées dont on voudra bien m'honorer.

MANUEL TYPOGRAPHIQUE.

PREMIÈRE PARTIE.

LA GRAVURE,

OU TAILLE DES POINÇONS.

POUR être un bon Graveur de Caractères, il faut être Typographe, c'eft-à-dire, favoir tous les détails du méchanifme de la Fonderie & de l'Imprimerie, afin d'y affujétir fon travail. Maitre de l'art, le Graveur doit tout prévoir dans la fonte & dans l'impreffion. C'eft par-là que les Simon de Colines, les Garamond, les

A

special typeface for the Imprimerie Royale's own use, the famous Romain du Roi. It was first used in the book *Médailles sur les Principaux Événements du Regne de Louis le Grand*, published in 1702, of which Morison reproduced four full pages in his folio *Four Centuries of Fine Printing*, and of which he wrote 'no book between the Gutenberg Bible, the 1457 Psalter and the Kelmscott Chaucer is comparable'.

The story of the committee and the lengthy researches into type design in connection with the Romain du Roi are described by André Jammes in a superbly illustrated article in the first number of the London *Journal of the Printing Historical Society*, 1965. The italic of the Romain du Roi was in fact the first 'sloped roman' – a concept which André Jammes points out was revolutionary and 'precedes by more than two centuries the theory put forward by Stanley Morison in the *Fleuron*, in his article "Towards an ideal italic".' The Romain du Roi was, indeed, as Jammes says, 'a reflection of the splendour of the reign of Louis Quatorze' – it was a great national achievement, the result of collaboration between scholars, bibliographers, scientists and artists – and it was the precursor of France's greatest contribution to type design, the so-called 'modern' face, perfected by the Didots. This was a typeface (and this was where many would say that the French went wrong) not based on the pen or the graver but on logic, or theory, with hairline serifs drawn with a ruler: the typeface chosen by Bodoni as his model, which became eventually almost the standard face for nearly all French book printing. In the opinion of most typographers in Britain and America today (I hope), the 'modern' face remains less legible, less graceful, than faces like Bembo and Caslon and Times, with bracketed or gently curving serifs.

France's next great contribution to typography was the invention of the point system, proposed and demonstrated by Pierre-Simon Fournier le Jeune in his *Manuel Typographique* in 1764-66, of which volume one was a manual on typecutting and founding, volume two a specimen which included over 100 alphabets, and a beautiful demonstration of the uses of typographical ornaments.

During the nineteenth century, it was book illustration that flourished in France: we think of Delacroix, Gavarni, Johannot, Daumier, Grandville, and Doré rather than of individual printers. And already in 1875, the painter Edouard Manet had entered the world of book illustration with his four lithographs for *Le Corbeau*, Mallarmé's translation of Poe's *The Raven*

86 DE LA JUSTIFICATION, &c.

a eu le bonheur de réussir, son ouvrage peut passer à la postérité la plus reculée dans le même point de perfection, sans jamais se corrompre ni s'altérer, parce qu'après avoir fait un long usage des matrices, on pourra les faire renaître de nouveau par le moyen des mêmes poinçons ; en cela bien plus heureux que le Graveur en taille-douce, qui, après l'impression de deux ou trois milliers d'estampes, est obligé de retoucher sa planche, & enfin de l'abandonner comme inutile. Les Caractères de fonte, au contraire, renaissent comme d'eux-mêmes, & font reproduits à l'infini pendant des siècles entiers par l'art de la Fonderie, dont nous allons voir le détail.

DE LA FONTE
DES CARACTÈRES.

SECONDE PARTIE.

L'ART de fondre les Caractères d'Imprimerie, qui est la seconde partie de la Typographie, exige de celui qui l'exerce des connoissances & de l'industrie. Il peut ignorer la Gravure, puisqu'il s'est écoulé des demi-siècles entiers sans qu'il se trouvât un seul graveur de Caractères en France ; mais il doit savoir au moins la manière de justifier les matrices, & posséder la théorie de l'Imprimerie, pour assujétir son travail à cette troisième & dernière partie, qui est le complément de l'art & le point de vûe du Graveur & du Fondeur. Son ouvrage doit être livré à l'Imprimeur dans toute sa perfection, parce que celui-ci n'y peut

– the book that is considered significant, rather than Delacroix's earlier incursions into book illustration by lithography, as the beginning of the French movement in book production known as the 'livre d'artiste' or the 'beau livre'.

We have seen that the revolt against declining standards in commercial printing at the end of the nineteenth century was shown, in England, Germany, Holland, and the United States, by the setting up of numerous private presses, and by the entry of architects and artists into type design. In France there were no private presses, but artists and sculptors began making their own plates for books. The demand for something better in book production than was available commercially was met by clubs of bibliophiles, who commissioned books to be made in limited editions for their members. Gordon Ray (*The Art of the French Illustrated Book*, 1982, p.373) lists eight such clubs, founded between 1874 and 1908, and pointed out that very few people today have ever seen their books, since the printing quantities were limited to the membership, which very rarely exceeded 100, and was often less. In 1893, Maurice Denis made 30 lithographs for André Gide's *Le Voyage d'Urien*, printed in an edition of 300 copies, and in 1898 there appeared what Ray calls 'The one substantial book illustrated by Toulouse-Lautrec', Georges Clemenceau's *Au Pied de Sinai*, in an edition of 380 copies. In 1900, Ambroise Vollard published the first of his great livres d'artiste, *Parallèlement*, by Verlaine, with lithographs by Bonnard, and printed, with the poems nobly set in Garamond italic, by the Imprimerie Nationale (the erstwhile Imprimerie Royale) in an edition of 200 copies. The manager of the Imprimerie Nationale, when he agreed to print the book, apparently did not read it and thought from the title *Parallèlement* that it was something about geometry.

When the book was published and seen to be what it was (the parallels were human bodies) the Ministry of Justice demanded that all copies be recalled, saying that it was inadmissible for a book banned on moral grounds to appear with the arms of the Republic on its cover. But a compromise was reached: it was issued with a different cover and title-page – and it still failed to sell. It is now of the utmost rarity and is recognized as a great work of art.

When the art dealer Vollard, followed a few years later by Kahnweiler, continued to commission artists as great as Bonnard, or Picasso, or Derain,

Ton corps dépravant
Sous tes habits courts,
— Retroussés & lourds,
Tes seins en avant,

Tes mollets farauds,
Ton buste tentant,
— Gai, comme impudent,
Ton cul ferme & gros,

Nous boutent au sang
Un feu bête & doux
Qui nous rend tout fous,
Croupe, rein & flanc.

Le petit vacher
Tout fier de son cas,
Le maître & ses gas,
Les gas du berger,

40

A page from Verlaine's *Parallèlement*, with a lithographed illustration by Bonnard. Published by Vollard, Paris, 1900. Reduced. See Gordon Ray, *The Art of the French Illustrated Book, 1700 – 1914*, 1982: many references and reproductions.

or Matisse, or Rouault, or Rodin, to illustrate books with original prints, the results tended to make other illustrated books look feeble – how could it be otherwise? How can you compare Matisse with, say, Kate Greenaway – or even Cruikshank? But it is also true to say that many of these books were not really books at all, but collections of plates, just as was the most monstrous book of all time, *The Birds of America* by J. J. Audubon, of which a man can hardly lift one volume – and there were four. This was where, in the opening years of the twentieth century, the genius of France was being exercised in book production, rather than in typography. But what was going on at this time in French typography?

It has been said that a poem by Mallarmé, 'Un coup de dés jamais n'abolira le hasard' ('The throw of a dice will never eliminate luck') published in 1897 – and which incidentally was published in England and not in France – was 'the first shot to awaken the spirit of the modern book'.

Mallarmé, an extremely intelligent and sensitive man, was thinking about how to use type in his day to communicate his ideas: he used the white paper itself as a means of expression. But I read that Valéry, one of Mallarmé's disciples, said of him 'He sought to elevate the page to the starry heaven' – and that, I fear, takes him beyond my ken.

Then there was the publisher Edouard Pelletan, who between 1896 and 1912 published some 70 books based on a very conscious and at the time much publicised aesthetic, which seemed to owe quite a lot to William Morris and the Private Press movement. Pelletan's books seem to me today to be very good, but no better than many books being designed at that time in Britain, Germany, and the United States. But mention must be made of two artists who designed typefaces which Pelletan used in his books: Eugène Grasset and George Auriol. Grasset (1841–1917) was trained as an architect, but worked in Paris as a designer and decorator. As a poster artist, Ray says 'he was ranked with Chéret and Mucha in contemporary esteem'. Auriol (born 1863, died 1936) was an illustrator, poet, writer, and a prolific designer of lettering, bookplates, monograms, and symbols: he designed a monogram for Cadbury's chocolate, and also the characteristic lettering used on the spines of the very attractive books published in Edinburgh at the turn of the century by T. N. Foulis.

The typefaces designed by Grasset and Auriol were art nouveau, and they offended Morison – and were summarily dismissed by him in his book on *Type Designs* in 1926. They offended Morison, and they may offend us, because they were designed not with a pen, but with a paint brush – and, particularly in the case of Auriol, a very blobby paint brush – as indeed was much Chinese and Japanese calligraphy.

Grasset's and Auriol's types can be seen and appreciated most easily in three remarkable volumes compiled by the French printer Francis Thibaudeau – *La Lettre d'Imprimerie*, published in two fat volumes in 1921 (dedicated to George Auriol) and their sequel *Manuel Français de Typographie Moderne*, published in 1924, dedicated to Grasset and to Georges Peignot, the type founder who had commissioned Grasset's and Auriol's type families, and who was killed in Flanders.

These three volumes by Thibaudeau are the first modern books on typography in French, and, are intended for a far more sophisticated audience than simply the trade printers. The *Manuel Français de Typographie Moderne* actually provides a series of progressive illustrations showing how to make typographic layouts by means of tracing from type specimens, and is the first book in any language to do so, beating Tschichold's *Typografische Entwurfstechnik* by some eight years.

The typography of Thibaudeau's books has to be seen to be believed. They are in total contradiction to the gospel of restraint preached, for example, by the Doves Press. When I first saw these books many years ago, being young and inexperienced and dogmatic, I could not take them seriously, and refused to buy them – for which mistake I was heavily penalized when I found them and had to buy them in London some years later.

The extraordinary thing is that in fact Thibaudeau's pages and types are very easy to read – if you try. The few pages that can be illustrated here do not and cannot do justice to a work which comprises over one thousand three hundred pages and is a profusely illustrated history of printing as well as an encyclopaedia of contemporary practice. Among other things, Thibaudeau proposes a detailed system for the classification of typefaces by their serifs, a system later taken up and improved by Maximilien Vox – of whom more later.

Thibaudeau is an important source for the study of some of the French attitudes to typography in the early years of the twentieth century: but his direct influence may not have been great. He died in 1925, the year after the publication of his *Manuel*.

George Auriol (1863–1936) as a young man.

George Auriol, c. 1920.

Georges Peignot, the great typefounder who commissioned type designs from Auriol. He was killed in 1915, and was followed by his son Charles.

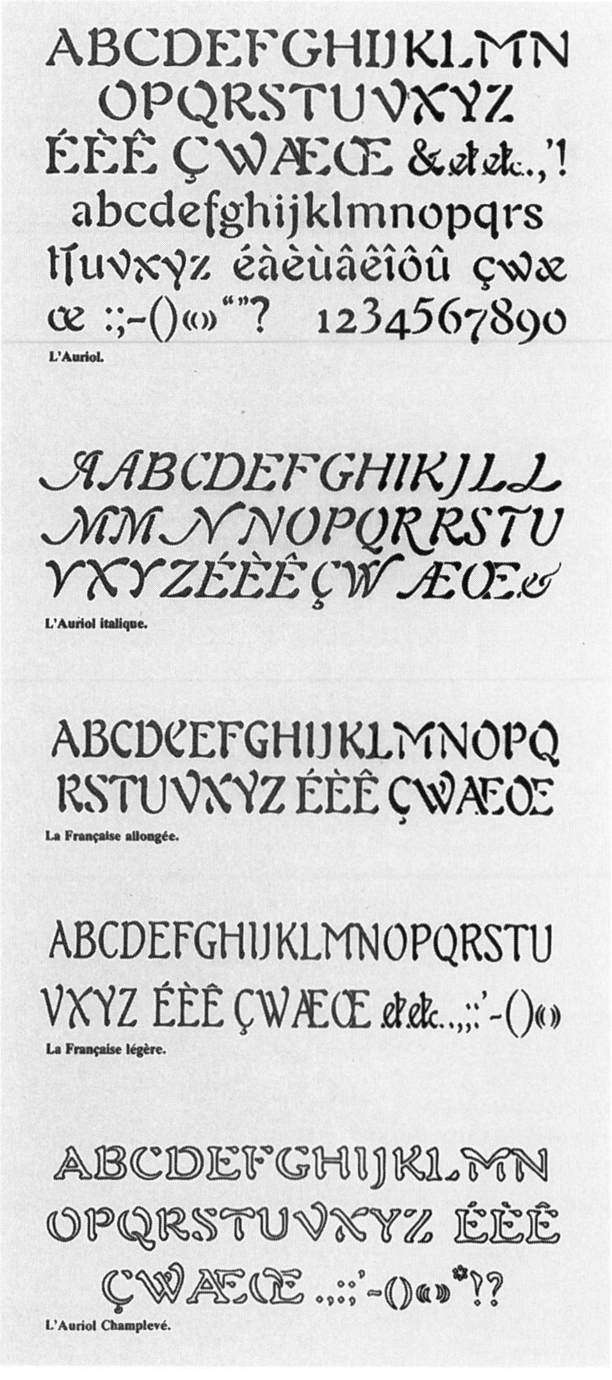

ABCDEFGHIJKLMN
OPQRSTUVXYZ
ÉÈÊ ÇWÆŒ &etet.,'!
abcdefghijklmnopqrs
ſuvxyz éàèùâêîôû çwæ
œ :;-()«»""? 1234567890

L'Auriol.

AABCDEFGHIKJLL
MMNNOPQRRSTU
VXYZÉÈÊÇWÆŒ&

L'Auriol italique.

ABCDEFGHIJKLMNOPQ
RSTUVXYZ ÉÈÊ ÇWÆŒ

La Française allongée.

ABCDEFGHIJKLMNOPQRSTU
VXYZ ÉÈÊ ÇWÆŒ etet..,;'-()«»

La Française légère.

ABCDEFGHIJKLMN
OPQRSTUVXYZ ÉÈÊ
ÇWÆŒ .,;;'-()«»*!?

L'Auriol Champlevé.

Five typefaces
designed for Peignot
by Auriol, of strong
calligraphic quality.

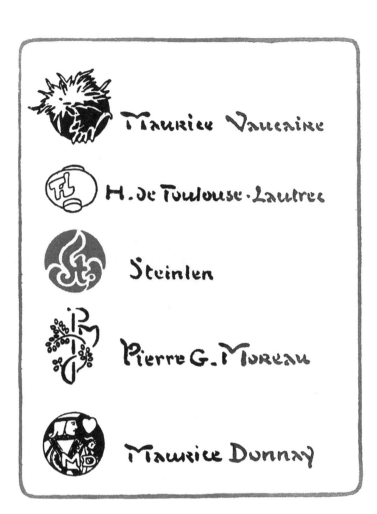

Five Art Nouveau symbols designed by Auriol, and the symbol he designed for Cadbury's Bournville chocolate.

The real influence on French typography, from 1920 onwards, has been exercised by Charles Peignot, son of the Georges Peignot who was killed in 1915, the type founder who commissioned the Grasset and Auriol types and many other better known ones – and to whose memory Thibaudeau dedicated his *Manuel*.

Charles Peignot took over control of the Deberny Peignot type foundry in 1919. He was a highly civilized young Frenchman, a friend of Jean Cocteau and well aware of what was going on in the art world of Europe. Peignot belonged to a group called the UAM – Union des Artistes Modernes – among whose members were four of the world's then greatest poster artists, A. M. Cassandre, Jean Carlu, Paul Colin, and Charles Loupot, and the typographer Maximilien Vox.

They were admirers of the Bauhaus and determinedly against anything that they considered backward-looking, which explains why they never had much interest in British typography, typified in their opinion by the Morison/Monotype programme of type revivals – which as far as they were concerned were all backward-looking. Deberny Peignot, who had already issued many fine and original typefaces, bought the rights from the Bauer type foundry of Paul Renner's sans serif Futura, which they re-christened 'Europe' and sold very successfully in France and French possessions. The two most notable contributions to new type design were both designed by Cassandre: they were 'Bifur', a daring display face in caps only, and 'Peignot', a modern uncial, not a revival, which was surprisingly successful but was never used for books (see p. 91).

In 1928 Charles Peignot founded a periodical, *Arts et Métiers Graphiques*. This was not, as one might have thought, a house journal to promote the sales of Deberny Peignot: it was never financed or published by them, but was a private venture financed privately by Peignot himself and a few friends. It came out six times a year and ran for 68 issues, ending only with the outbreak of war in 1939. In my opinion, *Arts et Métiers Graphiques* is far and away the most entertaining and visually satisfying graphic arts magazine ever published, and is typically French in the best way, just as *Graphis* is typically Swiss in the worst way.

For all its 68 issues it had the same format (about 311 × 247 mm) and the same editorial formula. It had five different editors, but was always under Charles Peignot's direction and inspiration. It had various cover

La Pratique
du
Croquis-Calque Typographique
en
20 Exemples.

*P*OUR une démonstration précise et générale des opérations du
croquis-calque typographique, prenons pour thème l'exécution
d'une carte oblongue de 13 × 26 douzes, avec le texte suivant :

 *L*E croquis-calque typographique de F. Thibaudeau :
fait l'éducation du Typographe ; réduit, pour l'Imprimeur et l'Editeur, les frais de maquette et de mise au point ;
et satisfait le Client, qui juge réellement de l'exécution de
son travail dans cette « épreuve avant composition ». ☐ ☐

C'E texte paraît bien chargé pour la surface indiquée ; il s'agit
néanmoins de l'y loger à l'aise, avec un cadre, de grosses lignes
de titres, un ornement assez important ; de ménager encore de belles
marges et de faire circuler l'air autour de tous les groupes afin d'en
rendre la lecture facile et la compréhension claire. ⬛ Le praticien
aura l'intuition que, pour arriver à ce résultat, le choix d'un caractère
allongé s'indique de préférence à un type large ; arrêtons-nous, en
conséquence, à la *Française légère*, dont nous avons la plaquette, à
l'aide de laquelle chacun pourra renouveler et contrôler l'expérience.

A page from Francis Thibaudeau's *Manuel Français de Typographie Moderne*, 1924.
Reduced.

compétence et le privilège d'obte- ∂℃ *Ce problème, complexe*
nir une main-d'œuvre parfaite. ∂℃ *à première vue, devient*
pourtant d'une solution assez facile si, par une initiation
progressive — ainsi que nous l'avons établi — on parvient
à mettre sur le même pied d'égalité techniciens et non-techni-
ciens devant l'examen du matériel typographique moderne
et de ses différents modes d'emploi. ∂℃ *Car il ne peut*
être question de rappeler dans ce Manuel les principes
de la pratique d'autrefois. Leur réédition ne pourrait
que détourner du but que nous poursuivons, sans profit
d'aucune sorte. Si, cependant dans certains cas, il est néces-
saire d'y avoir recours, on aura toute facilité de consulter les
ouvrages publiés sur la matière : le Manuel Roret, par
exemple, dernièrement mis à jour par notre ami Emile Leclerc
et dont les chapitres : Des observations sur la Composition, De la Mise en pages, De l'Imposition,
Des Journaux, Des Tableaux, De l'Algèbre, Des
Langues étran- *Ici nous traitons uniquement de*
gères, seront du *typographie moderne; nous*
meilleur conseil. ∂℃ *n'avons donc à connaître que*
les éléments et formules de disposition récemment introduits
dans la pratique et constituant ∂℃ *Notre classification*
exclusivement l'art d'époque. ∂℃ *des caractères et des*
ornements typographiques, l'exposé des différentes méthodes
de disposition ainsi que notre procédé de préparation des
compositions sont des choses neuves où tous ceux qui s'occu-
pent de typographie, professionnels ou profanes, ont à
glaner et à profiter, et sur ce point se trouvent à un même
niveau de connaissances. ∂℃ *C'est du reste le travail*
en commun que nous escomptons pour unifier le rôle de ces
deux nouveaux facteurs du métier, le préparateur de

XII

Above and right: two facing pages from the *Manuel Français de Typographie Moderne*, showing a typographic style (and text) that is like a conversation. Reduced.

82

copie et l'exécutant technicien, *cela par la réalisation*
du manuscrit typographique, *Car, pour tout*
de l'épreuve avant composition. *travail typogra-*
phique comportant la recherche de dispositions et de grou-
pements de textes avec une partie décorative, préalablement
à toute mise en composition, la constitution d'une maquette
s'impose aujourd'hui; les pratiques de la composition clas-
sique, uniquement basées sur la justification à axe central,
ne sont plus d'aucun secours. *Aussi, l'un des rôles*
principaux de notre Manuel *est-il d'apporter, de propager*
le moyen simple et commode de résoudre ce problème de
technique. Un exemple *Si un titre à* justification
permettra d'en juger. unique et à axe central
(ex. 1) *peut s'entreprendre simplement avec le* manuscrit
d'auteur en mains, *sans autre préoccupation que celle*
*d'observer les règles d'*alternance *dans la longueur des*
lignes, d'opposition des forces d'œil et de déterminer au
jugé le plus ou moins de chasse *des caractères, cette*
manière de procéder sera insuffisante quand, comme dans
l'exemple **2**, *il s'agira de répartir le même texte sur la*
même surface, ne fût-ce qu'en trois ou quatre groupes, de les
unir par quelques ornements, d'en assurer la stabilité et l'har-
monie générale. *Certes, le typographe capable d'exé-*
cuter la composition nº 1 montera, *c'est-à-dire disposera le*
mobile de la composition nº 2 et le consolidera sans aucun
supplément d'aptitudes; *mais il ne pourra exécuter le dit*
exemple **2** uniquement avec sa copie manus-
crite sous les yeux, **ainsi qu'il le pouvait pra-**
tiquer dans *Là se trouve le point de séparation,*
l'exemple 1. *là se révèle l'ajouté nouveau qui*
oppose *et* différencie *la* typographie classique *et la*

connaissons d'autre, à l'heure actuelle, que celui que la néces-
sité nous amena à innover il y a plus de vingt ans déjà et
dont une pratique journalière nous a permis de contrôler
l'efficacité. Ce procédé, durant cette période, subit les épreu-
ves de l'expérience et de la critique, et nul ne conteste aujour-
d'hui les immenses services par lui rendus à la pratique de
la typographie moderne par la diffusion de méthodes et
manières nouvelles de disposer, qui ont puissamment contri-
bué à l'élévation du niveau professionnel général. Il donne
surtout, à celui qui désire étudier la typographie et fixer ses
conceptions, la faculté d'apprendre seul et de réaliser lui-
même son éducation artistique et technique en exécutant,
sans matériel mobile, des compositions ayant toutes les
qualités, le rendu et l'efficacité d'une épreuve d'impression :
résultat qui permit l'organisation de tournois internatio-
naux au ren- ⬥ Le CROQUIS-CALQUE,
dement jusque- pour le nommer enfin, est l'ins-
là insoupçonné. trument dont nous nous servirons
et dont chacun saura vite apprécier la valeur éducative,
surtout si l'on a soin de lui conserver exclusivement son rôle
modeste de préparateur de copie, où rien ne peut lui
être substitué, étant en l'espèce juste ce qu'il faut être et rien
de plus. ⬥ C'est au rendement qu'on apprécie l'outil :
le Croquis-Calque, pour être adopté par ceux qui
l'ignorent ou qui le dédaignent, ne demande que l'épreuve
de l'expérimentation.

Another page from the *Manuel Français*. Reduced.

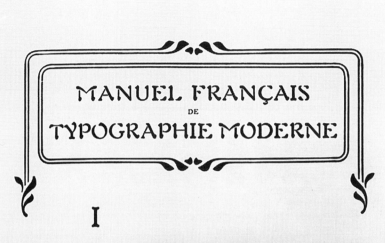

MANUEL FRANÇAIS
DE
TYPOGRAPHIE MODERNE

I

Bagage indispensable.

L'Imprimerie en raccourci.

*D*ÉFINITION. La *Typographie* est l'art de reproduire les textes au moyen de types mobiles, de grouper ceux-ci et de les acccompagner d'une ornementation appropriée à leur disposition et à leur usage. Par extension, on comprend sous le nom de Typographie la réunion de tous les arts qui concourent à l'Imprimerie.

*H*ISTORIQUE. Son invention est attribuée à Gutenberg, qui, à Strasbourg, vers 1436, se servit, le premier, de caractères mobiles. Pierre Schoiffer, son associé, vers 1454,

1

Page 1 of Thibaudeau's *Manuel Français de Typographie Moderne*, starting with his definition of typography.

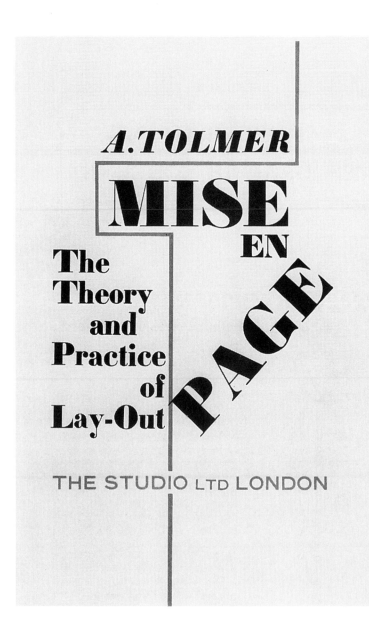

Title-page of Tolmer's *Mise en Page* ('Layout'), 1931. A French attempt to practise the 'New Typography'. Reduced.

The METHOD of ADVERTISING LAY-OUT

An advertising device: synthesis by means of detail. The accessories of dress-making, tape-measure, scissors and thread, in themselves suggest the dress that they have measured, cut out and sewn.

What in the last analysis is the most active rôle of modern lay-out ? We have seen that its most efficacious use is in publicity. But what is the method ? What is its function ? How exactly can a lay-out intercede with a man to induce him to buy a hat, a valise or a motor-car tyre ?

Since the end of all advertising is to sell goods, since its principle is to touch the susceptibilities of the purchaser, advertising psychology must deal primarily with the public consciousness.

It is not enough to say : « I intend to speak directly to the eye : I intend to strike the imagination of the public, to suggest a new want, a new desire, to impose my name and trademark on its memory, to give the public a taste for something it has never used before, and so to make it

change its habits, then to foment and sustain the suggestion that it should remain faithful to a choice made originally out of pure curiosity.» It is also necessary at frequent intervals to renew the arguments which are designed to appeal to the public and also to renew the method of presenting these arguments.

There is no technique of which modern publicity has not made use. Arrangements of cut-outs and cut paper have given a new direction to photographic advertising. We shall soon be seeing three-dimensional posters on the hoardings.

An opening from Tolmer's *Mise en Page*. Reduced.

Paris

A window opening on to Paris! Those who have known the bustle of the great capitals of the Old and New Worlds—Broadway, the Strand, Friedrichstrasse and the Prado—those who have lived in the grey atmosphere of Belgium, the white glare of Canada or the golden warmth of the countries of the sun, will be given an emotion unlike any other by the window which opens on to Paris, the capital of gaiety and pretty things.

As the freer conception of lay-out has made the printers' task incomparably more difficult, the printer himself can no longer afford to shut himself up within the accustomed limits. He must take an interest in every craft with which he comes in contact and in everything which may contribute to enlarge the scope of his expression.

The classical frame of this illustration has been wiled by the illustration itself. The layout of a modern subject requires a placing and movement appropriate to the style of the subject and movement mitigai it to harmonise with the regular format of the page.

An opening from Tolmer's *Mise en Page*. Reduced.

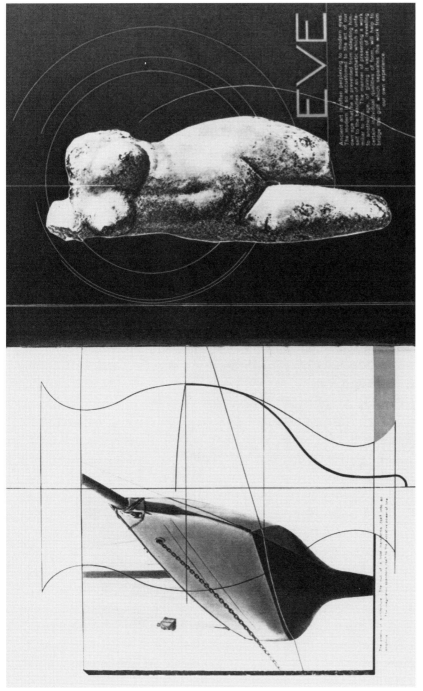

An opening from Tolmer's *Mise en Page*. Reduced.

designs, always lettered or typographic, never pictorial. The cover designed by Cassandre in 1931 was an early use of Victorian sans wood letter in large sizes, which I suspect caught Robert Harling's eye and inspired his superb covers for the periodicals *Typography* and *Art and Industry* a few years later.

Arts et Métiers Graphiques was characteristic for its extremely varied contents, but there was always an underlying formula. Apart from a few special numbers, on Photography, Caricature, Book Design, and Publicity, the magazine always began with a literary text, in prose or verse, treated in imaginative, experimental typography and printed on special paper as a separate section usually of four or eight pages. The first three of these texts were written by Paul Valéry, Valerie Larbaud, and André Suarez: thus the design of imaginative, creative words was always the first thing you came to, and it was never presented in Morisonian good taste, nor in pseudo-Bauhaus. After that came five or more main articles on every conceivable graphic subject, often with colour insets on special paper – and at the back of the magazine there were two regular features, 'L'Oeil du Bibliophile', showing book pages, and 'Actualité Graphique' showing posters and publicity – in which of course the work of Cassandre, Carlu and company was regularly shown.

Painting, sculpture and architecture by themselves were never subjects for *Arts et Métiers Graphiques*, but drawing, etching, and engraving, whether or not for books, were always given a lot of space; and what a wealth of wonderful drawings were available in Paris at that time for a magazine to show.

Arts et Métiers Graphiques was never specifically avant-garde, or doctrinaire; but it was visually alert, enquiring, amusing, open-minded. What did *Arts et Métiers Graphiques* contribute to the advancement of typography?

By existing for 68 issues, it must have reminded a few of its readers, some of whom must have been printers, that printing is an art and a matter for intelligent consideration and enjoyment. Apart from that, it covered, in a sort of way, what was happening in Europe during that period. It printed an article by Tschichold on the New Typography, it reprinted an article by Beatrice Warde on the work of Eric Gill from *The Fleuron*, vol. 7: it did not reprint, from the same Fleuron, Morison's article on *The First Principles of Typography* which I believe was never translated

NOUVELLISTES
PLAISANTERIE

ABCDEFGHIJKLMNOPQRSTUVWXYZ
abcdefghijklmnopqrstuvwxyz
1234567890

Two typefaces designed by A. M. Cassandre: Bifur, 1929, and Peignot, 1937.

into French until Fernand Baudin's translation appeared in the Brussels exhibition catalogue in 1966, thirty-six years after its first appearance in *The Fleuron* and long after it had been reprinted all over the civilized world in many languages.

Arts et Métiers Graphiques was however the only magazine ever to print – in translation – Morison's account of his railway trip on the footplate of the Flying Scotsman from London to Edinburgh, with three fine photographs of the locomotive, and – of course – the names of Morison, the engine driver and the fireman all spelled wrong. This was the only time that Morison's name appeared in the magazine as a contributor.

Arts et Métiers Graphiques's chief contribution to typography was that it gave a platform to Maximilien Vox. The difference between Vox and Morison as practitioners of, and writers on, typography, is the difference between French and British typography during the first half of the twentieth century. Vox was born five years after Morison, and died in 1974, seven years later than Morison.

Vox was born in Normandy as Samuel William Théodore Monod, and changed his name for political-religious reasons too complicated to go into here. His sons retain the name of Monod. Vox, before he became a typographer, was an artist, an illustrator and wood-engraver of very considerable talent and success – and also an author, editor, publisher, and translator. He illustrated works by Jane Austen, Kipling, and Dickens, as well as Voltaire; he edited Napoleon's letters and translated at least two books by G. K. Chesterton. The fact that he came to typography via illustration is significant and underlines the great difference between French and all other typography: French book design is based on illustration, while everyone else's came out of calligraphy. And calligraphy is – we may think – the truer basis of typography. But Vox and Peignot kept typography alive in France and provided a typographic background for the later achievements in type design of Excoffon, and Adrian Frutiger, the designer of Univers, who was born a Swiss, but who came to France to design Univers on the direct invitation of Charles Peignot.

I wish I had known Vox. He was a skilful and prolific artist and designer, an extrovert, a publicist and publisher, a frequent writer on typographic subjects for *Arts et Métiers Graphiques* and other periodicals, the author of the widely accepted Vox system of type classification, and – not

Maximilien Vox (1894–1974). Photo: Jean Dieuzaide.

least of his achievements – he was the founder and moving spirit of the École de Lure, a summer school at Lurs en Provence which became an important international meeting ground for designers of many countries.

When did typography as a profession come to be recognized in France? The answer to this question is conveniently provided by Vox. It occurs in an article he contributed to the special printing number of the London *Times* published on 29 October 1929, on 'Colour printing and typography in France' in which occur the words 'a new profession, that of typographical expert, is even now coming into existence'.

Here are three more utterances by Vox, which seem to me to show not only the sort of person Vox was, but also the sort of person a good typographer I hope will always be. They all come from an autobiographical article Vox wrote in *Arts et Métiers Graphiques* no. 45, in February 1935.

The first can be given conveniently in English: 'My only love is paper – printed paper. I eat it, I drink it, I dream of it: in it I find my best failures and my worst successes.'

Here is the second, first in French: 'Ce qu'il importe mieux de marquer, c'est ceci, la grande découverte, selon moi, et le plus sure, de mes vingt premières années d'activité graphique: que jamais, en aucune circonstance, on ne se donne trop de peine pour être intelligent ni pour faire confiance a l'intelligence du voisin' – which I translate as: 'My most important discovery, in my first twenty years as a graphic designer, and my greatest certainty, is this: that one must never – in any circumstances – put less than one's total intelligence into any job – nor ever underrate the intelligence of other people.'

And finally I end my Sandars lectures as Vox ended his article, with his words: 'Je ne peux travailler que dans la joie.'

'I can only work joyfully.'

Index